Curatorial Intervention

Curatorial Intervention

History and Current Practices

Brett M. Levine

ROWMAN & LITTLEFIELD
Lanham • Boulder • New York • London

Published by Rowman & Littlefield
An imprint of The Rowman & Littlefield Publishing Group, Inc.
4501 Forbes Boulevard, Suite 200, Lanham, Maryland 20706
www.rowman.com

6 Tinworth Street, London SE11 5AL, United Kingdom

British Library Cataloguing in Publication Information Available

Library of Congress Cataloging-in-Publication Data

Names: Levine, Brett M., author.
Title: Curatorial intervention : history and current practices / Brett M. Levine.
Description: Lanham : Rowman & Littlefield, [2021] | Includes bibliographical references and index. | Summary: "This book covers the history of intervention theory, initial research including interviews with thirty professional artists, curators, and administrators, working in Australia, New Zealand, and the United States with narratives that reflected both the prevalence of, and the inherent opacity within, curatorial intervention"-- Provided by publisher.
Identifiers: LCCN 2021000810 (print) | LCCN 2021000811 (ebook) | ISBN 9781538128718 (cloth) | ISBN 9781538128725 (epub)
Subjects: LCSH: Art museums--Curatorship. | Art museum curators. | Artists and art museum curators.
Classification: LCC N408 .L48 2021 (print) | LCC N408 (ebook) | DDC 708--dc23
LC record available at https://lccn.loc.gov/2021000810
LC ebook record available at https://lccn.loc.gov/2021000811

™ The paper used in this publication meets the minimum requirements of American National Standard for Information Sciences Permanence of Paper for Printed Library Materials, ANSI/NISO Z39.48-1992.

Contents

Preface vii
Introduction 1

1 The Interventionist Imagination 21
2 Aspects of the Almost Grotesque 45
3 Errata Minimalia 61
4 Reconfiguring Intervention 75
5 The Work Is (Not) on the Wall 91
6 Intervention Contra Engagement 105
7 Intervention Today 123

Bibliography 127
Index 135
About the Author 137

Preface

In a perfect story—the type you tell at dinner parties, the one that leaves listeners laughing to the point of tears—I would begin the exact moment I first wondered why gallery directors never, ever—it seemed—said no. The narrative arc would not revolve around some stack of unsolicited exhibition proposals that had arrived between stiff sheets of cardboard, sleeves of slides included. Instead, every word would float to each listener—on a cloud of sheetrock dust so thick that even a respirator would be insufficient, everyone who entered the space looked as if they'd been caught in an unexpected snowstorm or dusted—heavily—with confectioner's sugar, and, even weeks later, the light would still seem to have trouble piercing the impenetrable haze. The punchline? That the impetus for the creative cloud had absolutely nothing to do with technological innovation, and everything to do with the fact that the artist in residence had done her drawings on the gallery walls—with a router. Then, rather than pay to have new sheetrock installed, the simpler solution, though far less efficient, would be to have some gallery employee sand and fill the artist's fleeting creation.

For more than two decades, I've questioned—and qualified—just what the limits of an artist's exhibition practice might me. I've allowed artists to paint galleries floor to ceiling and wall to wall, installed and demolished temporary partition walls, and rooms within rooms. Some ideas seem great in theory, but in practice, maybe less so. Who would have foreseen the time-based performer who injured herself—while sitting inside a structure with no door. She would need to be lifted gently up and over a wall. Some years later, I asked the director if they might still happen to have footage of the incident. Every performer was videotaped as part of the artist's concept, to be replayed alongside a livestream of the performer the following day. Every experience led to similar questions. Why had I allowed the artist to create the work? Could it, or should it, have been changed? Would they have been open to creative compromises? Would the audience know?

Worldwide, curators and artists engage in similar dialogues every day. Physical, social, legal, and cultural limitations often mean that works have to be altered, or even not displayed at all. But this is not a chronicle of engineering challenges or unanticipated failures. As every curator will have experienced, sometimes the most significant and dynamic issue emerges after a proposal is accepted. Conflicts between plans, perceptions, and realities cause proposals to change. What happens later, if a curator or administrator has to request an artist to do the same? Does a request produce a collaboration? What might I, or an institution, need to say?

From the earliest moments of my professional education and training I saw differentiations between artistic intention and experiential outcome, yet often the causes and considerations remained vague. For audiences, these slight disparities, or small alterations, would likely have seemed insignificant. But for me, every change was vital. How did what the artist mean not quite translate into what viewers would see? And how, if at all, would that diversion be shared?

Over the course of my career, I have been as responsible for making these requests of artists as any other arts professional. That expansive painting? Its height is the largest that will fit through the gallery's double entry doors—on the diagonal. The width? It's the exact measurements of the gallery's feature wall. Made to the artist's specifications? Not at all. This is not to say that decisions like these occur without consultation, but any dialogues surrounding scale will always be fraught. "Why did the artist specify this scale?" Answer: they didn't. "Why did you want to work so expansively?" Hopefully, the artist will respond that creating a work of this size was a unique opportunity.

Experience, reflection, and analysis have all suggested that the artist-curator dynamic is not as transparent as it has always seemed, nor—even excluding curatorial authorship—is the curator as transparent as viewers are often led to believe. As a curator, arts administrator, and educator, I have always been motivated by those opportunities that make cultural and structural dialogues more apparent. I believe there are opportunities to redefine curatorial roles. And, I believe, the time for redefinition is now.

I have been fortunate to have worked across three distinct arts and museums communities—Australia, New Zealand, and the United States. This work would not have been possible if not for the many friends who have supported me throughout the process. Thank you to Professor Brad Buckley, who has championed my work over the course of my career. Thanks also to my mentors, in particular Tim Walker, who never ceases to combine insight with empathy. Kelly Carmichael, who has been a friend for decades; and Robert Leonard, former director of Artspace Aotearoa, with whom I shared an ongoing, tongue-in-cheek tally of exhibition concepts we categorized as "job keepers" and "job losers," and hosted what could be described as the best contemporary art salon in mid-1990s Auckland. To Ryan Daniel, thank you for your guidance on how best to combine the philosophical and the analytical. And thank you to everyone who, over the years, has always been intellectually available: Jessica Dallow, Mark Kessell, Ruark Lewis, and Ross T. Smith.

Most of all, my thanks and love go to Mindi Shapiro, a most formidable, frank, and funny reader and editor, whose endless patience, motivation, and inspiration ensured that this work came to fruition. This is for you.

Introduction

Imagine a museum that has a curator but is not open to the public. It has no viewers, makes no attempt to interpret its collection, and plans to make no further acquisitions nor to deaccession any works. If such an institution existed, as Kafkaesque as it sounds, one might argue that within it one would find the curator in their purest form: a keeper of objects. Against this imaginary, consider the Australian artist Peter Tyndall's series *A Person Looks at a Work of Art/Someone Looks at Something*. In this work, Tyndall encapsulates, perhaps ironically, the entirety of the problematics of curatorship. What he does with and through the—seemingly tautological—title is to partially detach the viewer from the act of viewing and, by doing so, from the activity of creating specific, situated meaning. In Tyndall's words, "someone looks at something," although one does not necessarily know if his two phrases are meant to be synonymous or to describe differing experiences.

Enter the curator. Here, I use the term reservedly, to mean those individuals focused predominantly on caring for, acquiring, exhibiting, and interpreting visual arts, media, and culture—and who emphasize the construction of experiences that operate within the parameters of an institutional or exhibitionary frame. Simply, they conceive of, design, display, and interpret exhibitions. My examination of curatorial intervention is not an attempt to redefine or resituate the meaning of curating, nor do I intend to place value judgments on the many manifestations of this practice today. Ours is an examination of individual versus institutional power, and of the complexities of experience and reception that result. Ours is also an attempt to redefine a historical misperception—one that suggests that the space a work of art occupies is delineated by artist and viewer (or audience) and that within this exchange there is no position or role for the curator.

The overarching question is not *if* curators have agency within the artist–audience exchange but rather if their mediations in advance of experience should be visible to the absent audience member. These mediations, as Boris Groys explains, problematize the artist–audience exchange to such a degree that audiences, as viewers, are compelled to evaluate which experiential frame they wish to operate within—a mediated curatorial frame or an unmediated creative frame.[1] In many ways, curatorial intervention emphasizes if and, if so, how *a spectator* or *the spectator* (think, the ideal spectator) experiences a work of art, rather than how every individual subjectively encounters works—and questions how the specific experience is mediated. This query forms the foundation of intervention theory. A more defined audience requires an even more nuanced response. The alternative is curatorial intervention, a construct, minus the specific terminology, is brought to the fore by theorists including Claire Bishop, who notes the significances of interconnectedness. In a discussion with Terry Smith, she remarks:

> We are always dealing with an ideal spectator—the one silently presupposed by the institution—rather than actual spectators in all their statistical diversity. But this way of thinking allows us to see the extent to which a museum's decisions about how to hang its collections are always profoundly ideological. When I presented these ideas recently to colleagues in other departments at my university, I was surprised to find that some of them never think about a museum's construction of meaning through the arrangement and juxtaposition of objects. It was news to them that art historians do a two-fold reading whenever we go to a museum: we look at the works, and we look at how the museum has arranged these works. We deploy two registers of looking simultaneously.[2]

In a 2016 artnet.com interview, "Art Demystified: What Do Curators Actually Do?," Hans Ulrich Obrist remarks to Henri Neuendorf, [3]

> Today, curating as a profession means at least four things. It means to preserve, in the sense of safeguarding the heritage of art. It means to be the selector of new work. It means to connect to art history. And it means displaying or arranging the work.[4]

Preservation. Selection. Collection. Display. Each of these four actions seems forthright enough, and each is deeply embedded in individual and institutional curatorial practices. True, there are works (or their elements) that can elude or deny preservation—a can of sardines exploding in Benjamin Patterson's *Hooked*, for example,[5] forty "leaking, smelling and fungus-harboring" potatoes in Victor Grippo's *Analogia I*,[6] or William Pope.L's 2,755 bologna slices for *Claim*, installed for the 2017 Whitney Biennial.[7] Living or decaying examples aside, one would agree that collections-based institutions regard preservation and acquisition as core values. Display is problematic to the extent that—as of 2009—museums and cultural institutions exhibited, on average, 4 percent of their total holdings.[8] The Metropolitan Museum of Art in New York, for example, holds two million works, including approximately 2,500 Old Master and 19th-century European paintings, and more than 15,000 works in its American wing.[9] If 4 percent of their holdings are on display at any one time, this would amount to 80,000 works. Finally, there is selection. If there were to be a problematic responsibility, it would be what Obrist identifies as the selection of new works.[10] Traditionally, works enter museum collections through purchase or donation. While the former offers institutional or curatorial agency, the latter less so. In many instances, museums are reticent to accept even significant works for a range of reasons—which may include the obligations of long-term care or the requirement that a gift be exhibited in a specific manner or to an agreed time frame. Examples of collections like these include the Lehman Collection at the Metropolitan and the Edlis/Neeson Collection at the Art Institute of Chicago.[11] Despite these constraints, and regardless of focus, curators have the capacity to drive collections, acquisitions, and presentations. After acquisition, display is the second-most significant responsibility a collections-holding institutional curator may have. Again, to quote Neuendorf, "curators decide how works are hung in galleries and how the viewing public experiences the exhibition, by researching how to show artworks in [an] art historically coherent and entertaining way."

And, as Jean-Paul Martinon observes, curators also fail. He writes, "All curators have at one point or another disappointed artists, fans, funding bodies, venues, followers, galleries, museums, subscribers and colleagues."[12] He describes how, in the 18th century, Charles–Claude de Flahaut, director general of Royal Buildings, spent thirteen years cataloging and preparing the Louvre collections, only to flee at the first signs of revolution. "D'Angiviller," Martinon writes, "is the archetypal failed curator." But perhaps Le Comte D'Angiviller is something else as well: the first interventionist. Martinon describes how he established methods for viewing, ordering, reading and interpreting, and selecting artworks, in other words, their reception.

For our purposes, the relevant definition of reception theory is one constructed from and synthesized through a range of theoretical writings, including those of Hans Robert Jauss, who was one of the first theorists to systematically structure reception theory's fundamental frameworks. Jauss also positions reception theory conceptually in relation to its historical and theoretical antecedents. He hypothesizes a triadic relationship of author, text, and audience in part by alluding to the ways in which an author and reader (and, hence, by extension, an artist and viewer) engage with texts or works. He writes:

> The historical life of a literary work is unthinkable without the active participation of its addressees. For it is only through the process of its mediation that the work enters into the changing horizon-of-experience of a continuity in which the perpetual inversion occurs from simple reception to critical understanding, from passive to active reception, from recognized aesthetic norms to a new production that surpasses them.[13]

Author and audience form two parties within a contested exchange. The work, seemingly shared, becomes a battleground. The reason the exchange is contested, and the reason there is a battle for its interpretation, is because the process is active. Michel Foucault, interrogating the function of the author, asserts in "What Is an Author?" that "this 'author-function' . . . is not formed spontaneously through the simple attribution of an individual. It results from a complex operation whose purpose is to construct the rational entity we call an author."[14] What Foucault suggests is that it is not merely enough to attribute the signifier "author" to an individual. Instead, that person must create or construct the conditions where the signifier—that being the work—reflexively attributes the signified author through experience. It would be simpler if this were attributed through rationalism, but this is not the case. In the current era, in which "curatorial constructionism" and "authorship" are becoming synonymous, Foucault's "author-function" defines a model of reception theory that would displace any construction of curatorial intervention that included the curator as well as the two other participants to the exchange.

Fundamentally, Jauss's formal structure of reception theory does not allow any frame that admits a third party. He constructs the aesthetic exchange as one within which experience occurs outside the potential frame of intervention, meaning that both intention and reception appear to operate as both closed and holistic. In his preface to *Aesthetic Experience and Literary Hermeneutics*, Jauss states:

> Aesthetic experience occurs before there is cognition and interpretation of the significance of a work, and certainly before all reconstruction of an author's intent. The primary experience of a work of art takes place in the orientation to its aesthetic effect, in an understanding that is pleasure, and a pleasure that is cognitive. Interpretation that bypasses this primary aesthetic experience is the arrogance of a philologist who subscribes to the error that the text was not created for readers but for him, to be interpreted by such as he.[15]

In Jauss's model, the curator therefore is always already absent, existing only in the hypothetical of potentiality as if the Heideggerian *allo agoreuei* of the editor were sufficient to insert the curator into the exchange. In fact, for reception theory to account for curatorial intervention as practice, it would have to become (or always already have been) a triad, and its invisible third participant would need to be made visible. The historical theoretical models for curatorial practice have failed to adequately allow for the agency of intervention precisely because there is this fundamental lack. That lack is (even the possibility of) the existence of the curator. And, since reception is often only mentioned as one element of the new museum experience, an alternative theoretical model that could both acknowledge and contextualize the curator's "intervention" has not yet been evaluated. As Jennifer Papararo, curator of the Contemporary Art Gallery, Vancouver, observes, "[r]eception is part and parcel of any exhibition,"[16] referencing and reinforcing the experience of reception, reinforcing the predominant theoretical duality of artist and audience, but again also only addressing the if, not the how. She continues, "[m]y aligning of artist and audience is not to put them on equal footing. The artist will almost always play a greater role in that equation"[17] Yet the issue is not the unbalanced power relationships between maker and consumer. Instead, it is those between maker, mediator, and consumer.

Yet, before proceeding further, it is also necessary to briefly outline what does not follow: intervention theory is not, primarily, an examination of reception. While intervention directly impacts reception—this is its *modus operandi* and its *sine qua non*—intervention theory operates relationally to the artist and resultantly to the audience. Intervention theory may alter an artwork or an artist's intentions relative to what can be received and the manner in which it is received, but it does not displace the audience experientially: what can be received *is* received. And, although intervention theory represents a vastly more comprehensive, and therefore more expansive, exploration of the work's journey from studio to spectator, it does not replace the experience of a work's reception. As a result, the story of a work's experience via reception remains; intervention theory simply fills in many of the exchange's blank pages.

The ever-increasing number of opportunities to experience art and the constantly shifting responsibilities that seem to oscillate between maker, curator, and receiver have captured the public imagination to such an extent that in November 2019 the Italian curator, theorist, and writer Francesco Bonami began to offer his perspective on curatorial practice in "Ask a Curator," a monthly column in *Art News* that provides insights and guidance about the profession. Perhaps, Bonami was motivated in part by the opportunity to reclaim some of the dignity and authority of a profession whose title had devolved into a synonym for any aggregation or compilation: music, socks, collectibles. As popular media have noted, everyone wants to be a curator—as we see in artsy.com's "Everyone's a Curator. That's Not (Always) a Bad Thing."[18] Of course, this apparently universal desire is not new. Similar articles decrying the emergence of "everyone" as a "curator" appeared in 2010 as "Everyone's a Curator, Now" (with comma) on the Smithsonian Institution Archives website, authored by the highly respected curator Marvin Heiferman, who has been responsible for transformational exhibitions, including *Talking Pictures* and *John Waters: Change of Life*;[19] in 2011, as "Everyone's a Curator Now" (no comma) at the Canadian site Maclean's;[20] in 2012, in "Everyone's a Curator!" on the *Baylor Digital Collections Blog*;[21] and, in 2014, as "Everybody's an Art Curator" in the *Wall Street Journal*.[22] If ever there were a title and concept more shopworn, and more regularly heralded as a cultural and critical harbinger, this would be it. Throw in a reference to the etymology of *to curate*—the Latin word *curare*, meaning *to care for*—and a standard framework for many texts on the emergence of quasi-curatorial practices is almost complete. Fortunately, Kelvin Browne, today the CEO and executive director of the Gardiner Museum, at the time of his remarks on staff at the Royal Ontario Museum, remarked slyly, "The concept of 'curating' your life is just an excuse for high-end consumption," he says. "It's pretending that buying stuff and putting it together is meaningful, but it's not."[23]

In fact, in 2016 Bonami had chronicled what one could term the "death of the curator," replying to an interview question that one goal of art was to dispel visions of mortality, or, in his words, "it's still needed by society because of its content and the story it's able to tell in order to make all of us forget that we do have—sooner or later—to die."[24] Despite his laconic reference to mortality, Bonami intimated that curatorial practice was still very much alive.

So, in 2019, the Metropolitan Museum of Art went so far as to attempt to contextualize this new curator in alignment with the museum profession by publishing an article outlining curatorial responsibilities. Titled "What Is Curating? See Why More and More People Are Interested in Becoming Art Curators,"[25] the article defined key curatorial roles: selection, organization, presentation. What is less important, apparently, in the Met's framework? Contextualization. Yes, "the color of the walls" and "the way each work of art appears from various angles" are significant. And, yes, it is important to consider the various levels of audience response—whatever they may be, as they are not chronicled. Missing from the dialogue? Intentionality. While a later quote from super-curator Obrist refers to a curator as a "sparring partner" and "a bridge," not every exhibition context requires a curator to position—or deflect—an artist's intentions.

Still, Jean-Paul Martinon writes in *Curating as Ethics* that "the focus on the visual—this old ocularcentric despotic trope of Western culture—is gone."[26] Not quite. The proliferation and hypersaturation of images across all media indicates that, in fact, ocularcentrism is alive and well. What Martinon would lead us to believe is that the mausoleums of art and white cubes of experience are no longer central to the experience. He may well be right—and in the face of a pandemic, these opportunities will certainly decrease—but the formal and formalized experience of viewing art will still occur to the greatest extent within the canonization of the museum sector, and through the materialization and realization of works within its confines.

In many ways, the Metropolitan Museum's desire to constrain—or at least contain—curatorial practice mirrored a conundrum that had been percolating for years. In the *Wall Street Journal*'s 2014 article on the concept of community as curator, for example, the subhead read, "As more art institutions outsource exhibitions to the crowd, is it time to rethink the role of the museum?"[27] Apparently not, according to Helen Molesworth, then the chief curator of the Museum of Contemporary Art, Los Angeles. She remarked:

> You're left with 10 paintings that may or may not make sense together, or may or may not be interesting together, or may or may not teach anything about the history of art—it's not the stuff of knowledge or scholarship.[28]

On many levels, Molesworth is correct. This approach, which might best be termed open-source curating, doesn't displace a curator; it merely quiets *the* curator as the singular, authoritative, traditionally formally qualified expert entrusted with the interpretation and contextualization of complex works for diverse audiences. Molesworth is also correct in her observation that collective or communal approaches to curating may blunt, or fail to connect, the many intricacies that emerge from deeply researched interpretations of works of art. A curatorial collective may connect Jackson Pollock's *Blue Poles* with Thomas Gainsborough's *The Blue Boy*—the first point of similarity between the two works is their common appropriation of the adjective "blue." But, despite the potential to connect Gainsborough's frenetic background brushwork with Pollock's gesture, there is a deeper narrative to be developed by investigating the extent (if any) to which Pollock's teacher Thomas Hart Benton was inspired or influenced by Gainsborough. Their shared focus on figuration could well have been a conceptual linkage that a "choose your favorites" approach to curation is likely to overlook.

These collective approaches to curatorial practice could well have informed Bonami when, in January 2020, his column has a response to a question concerning what a curator might notice about an exhibition that an audience might not: "The selection of the artists or the selection of the works. These are not just details, and yet a general audience can very rarely grasp what led to those selections, other than the general idea of the show. Also, shipping and insurance costs, pleasing a particular dealer or collector, refused loans, etc."[29]

Bonami framed his analysis using significant issues that traditionally fall outside an audience's purview: artist and artwork selection, costs, and the intricacies of the contemporary art world. Given the impact each factor has on exhibitions, Bonami's assessment is accurate. Audiences often experience exhibitions with little to no context concerning why a curator has selected particular artists or works, and, though budgets and expense reports may be available from public institutions through Freedom of Information requests, audiences rarely see the range of costs associated with mounting exhibitions. Instead, they receive a steady diet of ever-escalating artwork values, from Leonardo da Vinci's $450.3 million *Salvator Mundi* to Vincent van Gogh's $82.5 million *Portrait of Dr. Gachet*[30] or Jean-Michel Basquiat's $110.5 million *Untitled*.[31] These prices create an impression with many arts viewers that works such as *Salvator Mundi* are imperative for a transformative museum experience or a successful exhibition, and for expansive audiences to view. What is the perception of costs associated with contractual and logistical considerations, such as framing, crating, and shipping, on the experience of a work of art by comparison? Negligible.

Several months later, in May 2020, the legendary curator and art historian Germano Celant died of complications from COVID-19. Renowned for exceptional exhibitions and catalogs, Celant will be remembered for insightful projects from his *1997 Venice Biennale* (although reviews were lackluster)[32] to *Roma-New York 1948–1964*. Professionally, Celant was an iconoclast, as willing to anticipate the future as he was to reposition the past. Upon his passing, Bonami penned a remembrance in *Art News*. Two passages stand out. In one, Bonami begins, "I knew Celant changed the way art was made and looked at, and the way curating was done altogether," before concluding his commemoration thus: "You must give Germano Celant this: he was able to build up an uncompromising curatorial vision that never once weakened. As a curator, he felt he could do whatever [the] hell he pleased, and so he did. He was, after all, Germano Celant. If not a god, he was for sure one of the last, if not the last, great mythmaker of the 20th-century art world. He will be missed."[33]

"A god. The last great mythmaker." Pause, for a moment, to consider the power and implications of Bonami's assessment. We are speaking of Celant, posthumously, as a curator—not an artist—situating artists and movements, and manufacturing art history, from a seemingly unassailable position.

In 1994, *The First* (and what will transpire to be the only) *Artspace Open* publishes a call for artwork submissions. The exhibition invites residents living within the South Sydney City Council's boundaries to offer as many as three works to be juried. The curators are three highly respected Australian artists—Chris Fortescue, Susan Norrie, and Eugenia Raskopoulous.

Several hundred works are entered. Once the art is onsite, the curators share that, rather than make subjective judgments that will determine inclusion versus exclusion, they propose to install everything. The Artspace floorplan consists of an entry gallery bisected by glass double entry doors leading to the front desk and bookshop; a main gallery, entered via the entry gallery and through an opening to the left; and a smaller gallery, through a similar opening on the right.

The installation was unexpected. There were three pieces in the entry gallery—one work per wall. The main gallery was filled with submissions by well-known contemporary artists, hung in a linear hang. Two dozen—or fewer works—were on display. Finally, the smallest gallery held the remainder—stacked edge to edge, wall to wall, and floor to ceiling—salon style. One might recall here Brian O'Doherty: "The way pictures are hung makes assumptions about what is offered. Hanging editorializes on matters of interpretation and value, and is unconsciously influenced by taste and fashion. Subliminal cues indicate to the audience its deportment."[34] Cue and value—rather than hue and value—emerge in the visual constructs of the exhibition.

As Australian artists, critics, and curators will remember, in 1981, the journal *Art & Text* launched, accelerating discussions surrounding antipodean contributions to postmodernism and critical theory as well as situating the country within a larger international context. While many international arts journals were exploring similarly situated theoretical questions, the Paul Taylor and Paul Foss edited periodical *Art & Text* set the tone for Australian analyses of international contemporary art—and brought the lens of poststructuralism into focus for a far more broadly based arts audience.

As an intern, contextualizing the irony of salon-style installations as postmodern interventions meant pivoting away from a laconic egalitarianism that purportedly positioned wider Australian culture. Struggling with the installation's subjectivity, I asked Artspace's administrator, "How can we do this?" His response: "We do it this way because we can." Can and do.

Two months later, *Primavera 1994: Young Australian Artists* opened at the Museum of Contemporary Art, Sydney. Curator Natalie King outlined how the exhibition "investigated the way the museum's ensemble of art, architecture and installations orchestrates the viewer's experience. In different ways [the artists] utilize tools of display, arrangement and presentation in order to comment on the museum's desire to construct meaning."[35] Her description of David O'Halloran's *The Sound of the Box Being Made* is a reference to Robert Morris's *Box with the Sound of Its Own Making*. King remarks:

> O'Halloran's playground of museum building blocks, smooth and perfect, present a constellation of candy-coloured objects, with matt surfaces. The vitrine, donation box, museum seats, sloping information panels, plinths and architectural structures are abstracted and sculpted into an arrangement of lolly-like objects. . . . [A]s vessels, they are closed forms, seductively smooth formalist structures.[36]

When Morris constructed *Box with the Sound of Its Own Making*, he took the formalism of a plinth and reanimated it through his transubstantiation from an object to a work of art—in part by combing the visible object with an audio recording of its construction. Morris's *Box* operated indeterminately—the museum's context constructed its aesthetics as much as its content positioned its reception. *Box* may be read as plinth, but there is no necessary impetus to do so. With O'Halloran's works, however, the artist has already reappropriated the formal language of museum preparation and installation—the plinth, the information panel, the vitrine, the donation box—to blur the distinctions between institution as art and object as intentional element within a space of display. King anticipates that the museum will emerge as a contributing element to the experience of the works, just as the curators of the *Artspace Open* did at the instant each agreed to the all-inclusive exhibition framework.

Perhaps both O'Halloran and King sought to contextualize these works in an oscillating relationship to the viewer. Writing on Constantin Brancusi, the art historian Anna Chave has outlined how a number of his sculptural bases were essentially indeterminate: one and many objects, with differing values, simultaneously or consecutively. Brancusi was known to use a similar object for multiple purposes—his vertical and inverted tapered cubes called "zig zags" stack together to fill multiple roles from the plinth for a wooden cup in *Child in the World* (1917) to a sculpture in the small *Endless Column* (1918) and, then, as a larger object on a pedestal in his Paris studio before being realized as a monumental construct of verticality for the *Endless Column* at Tirgu Jiu. As Chave observes, "By making a sculpture that supported itself, or a base that was sculptural, Brancusi subverted the hierarchy of objects inherent in the mounting of sculpture."[37]

The indeterminateness of the base as object creates an opportunity for curators to intervene in the construction and presentation of Brancusi's works. While this seems problematic, in fact many of Brancusi's original bases are no longer associated with their sculptures, having been deemed distinct—and severable—from the art object. Brancusi disagreed, observing, "The pedestal should be part of the sculpture. Otherwise one should do away with it completely."[38] Reuniting the concrete object with a detached pedestal or base then becomes a matter of either a reproduction based on photographic documentation or a curatorial intervention based on informed perception and construction.

Immediately, uncertainties emerge regarding both the transparency and the agency of these actions. This is not so much a question of occurrence, but one of value. Questions including "Is the agency transparent?" and "Is the decision legitimate?" arise because of their dialogical curatorial intention. A pivot from artistic construction to curatorial intervention a priori means that this fracture forces the work to either deviate from its reception or be subsumed altogether, shifting the artist's communicative intent. "A need to produce mutual understanding between speaker and hearer,"[39] or, in this situation *either* between artist and audience *or* between curator and audience illustrates that both are mutually exclusive. Mediated reception cannot harken back to the real artistic intention. As a result, the linear trajectory from artist through curator to audience and meaning become fraught at best, nonexistent at worst. As Ellen Mara de Wachter wrote in 2018, "Curators tend to come up with conceptual, historical or formal frameworks within which to show art works, serving the artists' original intentions more or less faithfully; and artists have to be willing to see what happens to their work within those contexts. But while the intentions of curators and artists often overlap, the ground they hold in common is fragile and can be susceptible to expedient or ideological takeovers."[40] At first glance, it may be difficult to comprehend how a statement as seemingly innocuous as "because we can" is imbued with such power, but in a diagram of the artist–curator relationship, these three words are exceptional.

In that instant, "because we can" embodies a *why*, a *whom*, and a *what*—autonomy, agency, and power—none of which are contextualized by any corollary curatorial transparency. In one sense, this becomes an inquiry into agency-driven negotiation under the guise of decision-making. As Clas-Otto Wene and Raul Espejo remark, "The difference between strategic and communicative actions can be described in terms such as inducement versus understanding, winning the argument versus dialogue, and informing versus openness to discourse."[41] If so, this differentiation causes an instantaneous shift, one that marks the transition from artist-driven intentionality to curatorially mediated interventionality. Once mediated, an unencumbered artist–audience exchange becomes a chimera. Instead, intentionality and interventionality—mediated or unmediated—become the only two operational structures for exhibitions, and this schism remains to this day. At one pole, a residual frame of reception theory situates any encounter with art within the problematics of intentionality to reception. This perceptual narrative of reception theory—anchored firmly within the constructs of theorists, who include Hans Robert Jauss, Wolfgang Iser, and Roman Ingarden—creates a multiplicity of challenges when overlaid on the visual arts. At the other pole lies a wholly alternative experiential framework, a model that resites and resituates the apparently empty space between artist and audience, between intention and reception. A detour through reception theory illustrates this more clearly.

Still, what follows is neither accusation nor indictment. Curatorial intervention is not, primarily, a question of value. Instead, it is an operation that may influence values. Curatorial intervention destabilizes an existing dynamic—the artist–audience exchange—but its operation and outcomes may differ. Moreover, curatorial intervention does not operate more frequently in one type of exhibition than another. Whether group or solo, intervention occurs with equal regularity. What is problematic is the extent to which curators seek to insert their interventionist constructions between artist and audience as if it were a type of interdiction. This tendency, which curators discuss, although infrequently, was contextualized by Ugochukwu-Smooth Nzewi in a 2015 interview with Carolee Thea: "In the last few years the so-called independent curator has become increasingly powerful as a shaper of artistic trends and currents, I would not be the first to observe this state of things. But saying this tongue-in-cheek, some curators are fairly insecure around artists, and hence have the tendency to be dictatorial. Not infrequently the curator's personality or ideas take center stage instead of the artist or artwork."[42]

As importantly, the "curatorial" is also not my focus—although, as Maria Lind noted in 2009, "At its best, the curatorial is a viral presence that strives to create friction and push new ideas, whether from curators or artists, educators or editors. This proposition demands that we continue to renegotiate the conventions of curating."[43] Generally, the curatorial is expansive, whereas interventionism is insular. Each of the processes that bound the curatorial may be situated by curatorial intervention. But, prior to intervention's potential operation, it is as important to differentiate between those variables that structure the familiar artist–audience exchange versus those that situate the possible emergence of a dialogic and structural relationship that would include the curator. One area in which the curatorial excels, however, is in constructing interconnections and linkages that make outputs—exhibitions, publications, performances, events—signifiers of collaboration. As transit.hu observes, "The name itself is quite unfortunate, as it does seem to focus on the curator. Yet the concept endeavours rather to denote a particular way of working, involving many participants and different levels of collaboration."[44]

Lind's construction of contemporary curatorial practice situates artist–curator relationships as "curatorial pirouettes," which prioritize concepts, or "over-collaboration," which is a closely connected artist–curator dyad that produces new works.[45] Whereas today, curatorial studies programs and curatorial training produce graduates well versed in the concept of the curator-as-author; this propensity may well generate tensions between institutions and individuals. When discussing this dynamic, Lawrence Rinder remarked that the construct "hasn't gotten much traction in the museum world," and that this expectation—exhibition as personal expression—may well run contrary to a museum's other mandates, including audience engagement.[46] In a 2017 interview with Artnet.com, Lisa Phillips, Toby Devan Lewis director of the New Museum of Art, said of the museum's chief curator and artistic director Massimiliano Gioni, "He sees curating as an art form."[47]

The dyad artist–audience positions the traditional dynamic between object and experience. The experience is defined historically as intention and reception, conceptually anchored in a transferal. In its most reductionist form, the existence of this potential delineates reception theory and (according to Jauss) locates the artist–audience exchange outside a space of shared experience. Both the art object and its experiential exchange occur outside the subjects. Instead, reception theory constructs an encounter that structures and then reinforces a *lack* that each participant shares. The artist, having completed the work, releases it to the experiential sphere and withdraws; the audience, whether singular or plural, (generally) never encounters the artist. Instead, they encounter and experience the work—at which point they bring the totality of their interpretative resources and prior experiences to bear. To state the problem more simply, the audience never knows what the artist intends, and the artist never knows what the audience receives. Instead, what occurs is mediation, or, to interpret Marcel Duchamp—from the "expressed but unintended" to "the unintentionally expressed"—as the authors outline, either structuring the spectator's aesthetic evaluation.[48] As Jauss explains:

> It is only through the process of its mediation that the work enters into the changing horizon-of-experience of a continuity in which the perpetual inversion occurs from simple reception to critical understanding, from passive to active reception, from recognized aesthetic norms to a new production that surpasses them.[49]

There are two operations—one, an oscillation between constructor and interpreter, and the other a shift from passive to active. Yet, for these mediations to occur, each must infer the absence of a third party: the curator. Jauss's construction of reception theory—and the construction of reception theory in general—relies not on the invisibility of the curator but on the fact that they are just not there. Not absence; instead, nonexistence. Any other interpretation creates an impossibility because it would insert a third party within the exchange. For reception theory to function, it must operate within a duality, and its dialectic must be that of intentionality and reception. If there were a third variable to the equation—or a third contributor to the exchange—what construct would that possibly be?

Imagine if curatorial authorship could solve the puzzle. The construct of curators as creators has generated such interest within contemporary practice that an entire journal—*The Exhibitionist*—was grounded in and based on critical interrogations of these phenomena. In its inaugural issue, editor Jens Hoffmann remarked:

> In recognition of the set of operations and frameworks for the production and circulation of meaning that Foucault was keen to foreground, we concur that the curatorial process is indeed a selection process, an act of choosing from a number of possibilities, an imposition of order within a field of multiple (and multiplying) artistic concerns. A curator's role is precisely to limit, exclude, and create meaning using existing signs, codes, and materials.[50]

The Exhibitionist identified its theoretical genealogy by situating *Cahiers du Cinema,* and thereby auteur theory, as its intellectual forbearer. Yet such a hyper-focused emphasis on curatorial *authorship* had the potential to direct inquiries away from a more problematic occurrence: the opaque exercise of curatorial *authority*. For where curatorial authorship centers the construction of an exhibition, curatorial authority is instead primarily concerned with the operation of an exhibition's power. Whereas one constructs its narrative, the other defines its economy. The former defines the "what" and the latter, the "how."

Situating the curator within this role is not without problems in part because the emergence of the auteur–curator stands at odds with prior curatorial constructions that previously attempted to operate as transparently and neutrally as possible—leaving authorship and intention with the artist. And, while institutions today remain structurally defined and historically informed, the construct of curatorial intervention as praxis does not by necessity situate artist–curator exchanges moving forward.

Historically, with auteur theory and reception theory as its principal models, the artist–audience dialecticism (and didacticism) was welcomed as a model that offered an unfettered connection between the two. The dialectic functioned without synthesis, leaving the artwork in a void—always already severable from both intention and reception. Artist and audience may converge at the site of the object, but this simultaneous arrival would not equal synthesis. The object is like a ball in flight—thrown, but not yet having been caught. Alternatively, curatorial authorship would be third-party autonomy—rather than third-party synthesis—operating outside "intentionality" and "reception."

Reception theory is a mode of analyzing the artist–audience or object–viewer exchange. At a remove from the artist, the construction of meaning lies with the viewer, individuated and unmoored from the object. In these instances, "a mediated text"—including an artwork—"is separated in its production from its reception."[51] As significantly, reception functions by shifting the role of meaning-making onto the viewer, as opposed to the object. As Gretchen Barbatsis remarks, "there is an intention on the part of a producing agent—a painter, a director, a photographer—about how she wants a text—her painting, film, photograph—to be read and, further, that reading-viewers would approach these pictures 'expecting to find out.'"[52] Then, there is an expectation that there will be an engagement with an "other" that grounds the exchange within structural and philosophical frames. For reception theory to function, however, that other must be unmediated, must manifest as object-by-extension, as a transmutation of meaning within the experiential. If so, the emergence of the curator, and intervention's potential, would be moot—or, perhaps, mute.

Thus, curatorial intervention emerges as an institutional frame—as a viable critical method whereby works become experienced, their reception now being at one remove. In 1998, Michael Brenson identified curatorial intervention as one of five of the year's main exhibition themes, writing that "issues embedded in the exhibitions" included "respect for the intimate experience of art versus a belief in curatorial interventions that can make the artistic message, and sometimes even the intimacy itself, broadly accessible."[53] Brenson goes on to remark that "the increasing institutional awareness of the importance of the audience has made curators more visible as mediators between art and its publics."[54] Tracing histories of formalist additions and interventions can be tracked through the various manifestations of works such as Rachel Whiteread's *Water Tower*,[55] now owned by the Museum of Modern Art. There are many variations to the wooden structure—the dunnage—that originally supported her cast-resin work. In an essay on the challenges presented by altering *Water Tower*'s existing structure, architect James Middlebrook remarked, "The contextual significance of gravity within the artwork provided a clear design strategy for my task: the components to be added were thus organized with a design language to emphasize the structural nature of each condition. Efficient use of material was intended to minimize distraction from the tank's form. However, the visual physicality of the structure and its resistance to gravity was paramount, and the industrial aesthetic was intended to complement Whiteread's nostalgic portrayal of the tank element within the historically industrial skyline."[56] Here, the author conceives of, collaborates upon, and designs additions to the structural frame of Whiteread's artwork—intervention? Perhaps, but in consultation with the museum's curators, as well as the artist herself. As will be explored in depth further, intervention may be positive, neutral, or negative. Its sheer existence is not problematic—its manifestation is the measure.

Curatorial intervention revalues the dyadic artist–audience exchange. It restructures the artist-to-artwork-then-experience exchange from artist-audience, intention-reception, maker-viewer to artist-curator-audience, intention-intervention-reception, maker-curator-viewer.

Curatorial intervention's triadic construct—artist, curator, audience—proposes a model that can locate artistic and creative agency while simultaneously foregrounding issues of curatorial transparency, agency, and power.[57] Yet, how can existing artistic and experiential frames for art allow the insertion of a third party into reception's artist–audience dialectic—and how might the implications of this new structure to be understood?

Before proceeding, it is important to note that—despite occasional assertions to the contrary—the curator is not as to the artist as the editor is to the author. At the point at which the writer–reader exchange occurs—the book—the work of the editor has been done. The reader/receiver may then experience the work however they choose; they may read it in bright sunlight or in a dimly lit room; they may skim it quickly or pore over every word; they may use a bookmark or keep their place by folding a corner. The experience of the object is theirs. But an experience of an artwork is not the same, in most instances. Apart from encounters with outdoor sculpture or other experiential works, in many instances curators control not only the content of the exhibition but also its context; they may control the lighting, the color of the walls, the arrangement of the images, the inclusion or exclusion of pedestals, three-dimensional pieces, curtains, benches, or other enticements or obstructions, labels, flyers, publications, and more. So the encounter with the curator extends beyond the audience's preparations to experience the object. Unlike the reader's understanding of the editor *contra* the book, the viewer's engagement with the curator seems boundless.

However, a curator may construct a plausible narrative whether with the acquiescence of artworks or without them. Felix Vogel remarks, "today the artistic work creates a plausible justification for a curatorial thesis—a topic, a generalization, a classification, or just one combination and connection with other works that provide a framework of meaning—and in the extreme case is simply their illustration."[58]

What does "to intervene" mean? The *Oxford English Dictionary* defines this verb as to "[t]ake part in something so as to prevent or alter a result or course of events." The notion that disparate power relationships are a core construct of intervention is apparent. The example the OED uses states, "he acted outside his authority when he intervened in the dispute." And it is within this notion of disparate power relationships that the first suggestions of curatorial intervention can be found. Once outside the sphere of artists working solely with major, top-tier commercial galleries, many artists regard themselves as subject to the vagaries of curatorial power. This dynamic is described by curator Paco Barragán differently—as "soft censorship,"[59] which emerges as the outcome of negotiations between artist and curator—potentially. But "soft censorship" focuses on negotiation, not outcome. Barragán posits:

> The curator exercises indirect, or soft censorship, which forms a barrier between the artist and the public that rarely or never reaches the public sphere. After all, an exhibition only becomes a hard fact when it gets displayed to the audience. Before that it only exists as a mere possibility. Both the artist and curator engage in a dialogue of censorship of their own artistic works and curatorial projects in an act of self-censorship in which the conflicting rights of the artist and institution are being balanced to determine what can and cannot be censored.[60]

Instead, I would argue, and experience suggests, that the artist–curator dialogue is always already weighted in favor of the curator as institution. Despite the development of commercial gallery spaces as "quasi-museums," capable of mounting "museum-quality" exhibitions, in fact both visitor access and visitor familiarity remain focused on museums and related institutions. Exceptions exist—such as 80,000 visitors to a 2018 Yayoi Kusama exhibition at David Zwirner in New York[61]—but, overall, studies indicate that museum and gallery visitation is declining.[62] As a result, artists are less likely to jeopardize opportunities to reach an audience, particularly as the result of debating the works to be exhibited. As the Australia-based New Zealand Maori artist Ross T. Smith remarked recently, "curators have the ultimate decision, because it's their gallery. The curators are in control."[63]

Once a work is on display, it is not so much a question of soft censorship but instead self-censorship that resituates the curator at the site of intervention.

This perception represents one of many operations of curatorial intervention. Curatorial intervention takes many forms: curators may encourage artists to produce or reproduce certain works or types of works; curators may alter, amend, or change either the content or contexts of artists' projects; or curators may simply recontextualize artists' works—with or without their knowledge. And the frequency with which these three interventions occur appears to be astonishing.

NOTES

1. Groys, "The Curator as Iconoclast," loc. 1000. Groys writes, "The curator's every mediation is suspect: he is seen as someone standing between the artwork and its viewer, insidiously manipulating the viewer's perception with the intent of disempowering the public."
2. Terry Smith, "Interview with Clare Bishop," 142.
3. Neuendorf, "Art Demystified."
4. Ibid.
5. Dinoia, "When Art Is Alive, How Do You Conserve It?"
6. Ibid.
7. Urist, "How Do You Conserve Artworks Made of Bologna, or Bubble Gum, or Soap?"
8. Fabrikant, "The Good Stuff in the Back Room."
9. Metropolitan Museum of Art, "General Information."
10. Neuendorf, "Art Demystified," 2016.
11. Kaplan, "When Collectors—Not Curators—Dictate Art History."
12. Martinon, *Curating as Ethics*, 159.
13. Jauss, *Theory and History of Literature: Towards an Aesthetic of Reception*, 19.
14. Foucault, "What Is an Author?," 127.
15. Jauss, *Theory and History of Literature: Aesthetic Experience and Literary Hermeneutics*, xxix.
16. Marincola et al., *Pigeons on the Grass Alas*, 43.
17. Ibid.
18. Cohen, "Everyone's a Curator.
19. Heiferman, "Everyone's a Curator, Now."
20. Kingston, "Everyone's a Curator Now."
21. Ames, "Everyone's a Curator!"
22. Gamerman, "Everybody's an Art Curator."
23. Browne, "A Museum without Visitors Is Just an Attractive Warehouse."
24. Neuendorf, "Francesco Bonami Says Curators Are 'Self-Delusional' and 'Irrelevant' in Today's Art World."
25. Richman-Abdou, "What Is Curating?"
26. Martinon, *Curating as Ethics*, viii.
27. Gamerman, "Everybody's an Art Curator."
28. Ibid.
29. Bonami, "Ask a Curator: Francesco Bonami on Difficult Artists, the Decade's Biggest Art Flops, and More."
30. Muchnic, "Van Gogh Painting Sells at Record $82.5 Million: Art: 'Portrait of Dr. Gachet' Is Auctioned to a Japanese Gallery."

31. Pogrebin and Reyburn, "A Basquiat Sells for 'Mind-Blowing' $110.5 Million at Auction."
32. Greenberger, "5 Essential Exhibitions by Germano Celant, Late Curator Who Coined Arte Povera."
33. Bonami, "Francesco Bonami Remembers Late Curator Germano Celant."
34. O'Doherty, *Inside the White Cube: The Ideology of the Gallery Space*, 24.
35. King, "Primavera 1994."
36. Ibid.
37. Chave, *Constantin Brancusi: Shifting the Bases of Art*, 27.
38. Andreotti and Brancusi, "Brancusi's 'Golden Bird': A New Species of Modern Sculpture."
39. Claus-Otto Wene and Raul Espejo, 1999, "A Meaning for Transparency in Decision Processes." (NEI-SE--308). Andersson, Kjell (Ed.). Sweden, 407.
40. Mara de Wachter, "After the Nymphs Painting Backlash: Is Curatorial Activism a Right or an Obligation?"
41. Note 39, at 407.
42. Carolee Thea, "Nzewi, Ugochukwu-Smooth," 55.
43. Lind, "On the Curatorial," 103.
44. Esther Szakáks, Curatorial, in tranzit.hu, 2015. http://tranzit.org/curatorialdictionary/index.php/dictionary/curatorial/
45. Lind, "Why Mediate Art?," loc. 1318–22.
46. Rinder, interview with the author, 2016.
47. Elbaor, "Getting a Master's Degree in Curating Is All the Rage. But Is It Worth It?"
48. Stainforth and Thompson, "Curatorial 'Translations': The Case of Marcel Duchamp's Green Box," 3.
49. Jauss, *Theory and History of Literature: Towards an Aesthetic of Reception*, 19.
50. Hoffmann, "Overture," 29.
51. Barbatsis, "Reception Theory," 271.
52. Ibid., 273.
53. Brenson, "The Curator's Moment," 16.
54. Ibid., 18.
55. InVisible Culture, "Amending Rachel Whiteread's Water Tower: Infrastructure as Art, Art as Infrastructure." As the author remarked about Whiteread's work,

> "Described by the artist as 'physically present yet ephemeral,' the four-and-a-half-ton translucent resin form (cast from an actual water tank) had been designed to sit on a steel dunnage (support frame) structure, just like real water tanks on the roofs of the city. This structural support has been important in the display of the work at each of its locations. Although the resin component remained unchanged, the supporting structure has been significantly altered several times since the work was initially assembled in 1998. At its SoHo site, the dunnage was significantly taller than at the MoMA site. The original structure had two complete x-frame braces stacked vertically, and these were buttressed along one axis with diagonal braces. An access ladder was placed almost centrally along one of the longer sides. Overall, the volume of the support structure was at least twice as large as the tank itself. The level of detail and the black sinuous quality of the structural steel members, connections, and ladders contrasted with the smooth aesthetic of the tank form. The tank resembled a space capsule sitting on complex booster rockets amid the diagonally braced scaffolding of a launch pad, which communicated a sense of suspension or extension through expressive structure. This version of the structure possessed a Constructivist quality that was fitting for the industrial SoHo context."

56. InVisible Culture, "Amending Rachel Whiteread's Water Tower: Infrastructure as Art, Art as Infrastructure."

57. A similar structure, using the terminologies *agency, authority,* and *urgency,* form the foundation for Lorna Cruickshank and Merel van der Vaart's examination of curatorial practice in their 2019 article in Stedelijk Studies, "Understanding Audience Participation through Positionality: Agency, Authority, and Urgency." The correlation is agency/agency, urgency/transparency, and authority/power.

58. Vogel, "Authorship as Legitimation," 161.

59. Barragán, "The Curator as Censor (On Censorship and Curating)."

60. Ibid.

61. Corbett, "The End of Exhibitions? As Attendance Plummets, New York Dealers Are Scrambling to Secure the Future of the Art Gallery."

62. Ibid.

63. Ross T. Smith, interview with the author, 2016. There are two interviewees who participated in this project: Maori photographer Ross T. Smith and Black interdisciplinary artist Bayeté Ross Smith. Since each has Ross and Smith in their names, Ross T. Smith is hereinafter referred to as "Smith," and Bayeté Ross Smith is cited as "Ross Smith" or "B. Ross Smith."

ONE

The Interventionist Imagination

> The tarps are a bright, incongruously cheerful yellow stretched tight across gunmetal-gray stanchions. They don't reach the floor, and they rise only about two feet above eye level, so they don't cover much. You can easily crouch down to slip your head underneath or peek through the slits between the vinyl sheets. Beyond the passageway formed by the tarps, the monumental elements of the installation rise all around you, plain as day—the cinderblock walls, the two-story house, the guard tower, the trailers, the carnival ride, all compacted together in a claustrophobic, politically surreal borough of hell.
>
> —George Orwell by way of David Lynch[1]

We begin this story near its midpoint, in 2007. The artist Christoph Büchel has left the building, decamping to Europe for some unspecified period. In his absence, Joseph Thompson, director of the Massachusetts Museum of Contemporary Art (MASS MoCA), has made a series of difficult decisions concerning how best to proceed to protect the museum's interests, programs, and integrity—while at the same time attempting to continue working with Büchel in good faith.

Articles, essays, and letters emerge in the mainstream media—and precede as yet unfiled artist–museum litigation. The lawsuits generate hundreds of pages of documents that become part of the litigation's public record. Stories the correspondence contains reveal the depth of animus that emerges in the course of the artist–institution dispute and will chronicle a series of creative and collaborative conflicts to enraptured audiences and creative communities. MASS MoCA, its constituents, and the wider curatorial community will see the intricacies and intimacies of two overarching questions emerge: What exactly is curatorial intervention? And how, precisely, does it operate?

The narrative evolves because Büchel, the work's creator, has become disillusioned with how *Training Ground for Democracy*—his site-specific installation for MASS MoCA—is proceeding. Physically, some suggest, he appears to have abandoned the project, a perception that in 2007 is perhaps premature. Or, perhaps, his engagement with the work is not the sole issue. I prefix these observations with "perhaps" because, even throughout the course of the litigation that ensues, questions regarding both Büchel's and the museum's intentionalities will remain.

For every operation but chance (and some might argue for its existence there as well), intentionality lies at the center of the creative process. In *Training Ground*, this intentionality was evident in and through Büchel's actions. While more comprehensive facts of the saga are eloquently chronicled elsewhere, the Borgesian encyclopedia of objects that Büchel planned to weave throughout *Training Ground* deserves elaboration:

> Among the items installed were an oil tanker that had to be cut open and decontaminated; a smashed police car; a truck; a used mobile home; deactivated bomb shells; nine shipping containers; a shuttered local movie theater; and a 1,400-square foot, two-story Cape Cod–style house that was lifted out of the ground, sliced into four pieces, and reassembled. The museum ran out of money before they could obtain the 727 fuselage Büchel had asked for and continued to insist on.[2]

That fuselage. The fuselage will emerge as a creative, conceptual, and concrete work component around which theoretical, as well as legal, foils against Büchel's demands can be constructed. MASS MoCA is willing to engage, even should Büchel's creative aspirations exceed the museum's contractual obligations—and existing budget. One need only infer the sense of resignation in Joseph Thompson's voice as he chronicles one fruitless search to the *Boston Globe*: "Well, [the 727 fuselage] we couldn't come up with. But we looked into it."[3] Look into it they did. Documents, which emerge as exhibits in subsequent litigation, chronicle the specific steps MASS MoCA took in an attempt to acquire a plane's fuselage from an Arizona boneyard.[4] The *Boston Globe* article transforms public assessments of the as yet incomplete installation. Perceptually, the 727 fuselage comes to symbolize artistic and creative largesse. By specifying the fuselage, MASS MoCA infers, perhaps unintentionally, that the individual elements of *Training Ground* are severable one from the other.

A letter from Joseph Thompson to Büchel, contained in court documents, is even more revelatory:

> You hoped to enter the project through a circuitous aperture defined by a box office, concession stand, and fully rendered cinema, and we helped you devise that intricate path via an elevated projection booth. You hoped to build your work largely from sea containers instead of the simpler "fake storefront" construction technique of your original proposal and, at your urging, we agreed last summer to construct a 12′ x 24′ overhead door within our gallery to accommodate that new con-

> cept, and purchased, shipped and installed nine containers. You wanted imposing cinder block walls, and they had to be real, and high, and we built them, underpinning our galleries with steel when necessary to make that feasible.[5]

This is but half of Thompson's chronicle of—to the museum—completed tasks. Büchel disagrees. Trapped by the parties' inability to reach agreement—complete/incomplete, artist owned/museum owned, public/private, acceptable/unacceptable—*Training Ground* languished. Complex dialogues occurred. There, differing perceptions of artistic agency and curatorial intervention emerged. At the time, several museum administrators were sympathetic to MASS MoCA's predicament and their desire to present *Training Ground for Democracy* in some iteration. As Edgers related:

> Holly Block, director of the Bronx Museum of Art, was among the art-world officials who toured the show last month. "Open it anyway, as it is," Block said she told one of the curators. "Show it as a work in progress."[6]

Others disagreed. "That idea disturbs [Giovanni] Carmine, Büchel's sometime collaborator. "You wouldn't open a show of paintings if all the paintings are not on the wall," he said."[7] Perhaps not. But dynamic exhibitions are common. Creative additions—themselves artistic decisions—take a Yayoi Kusama *Obliteration Room* from an expanse of whiteness to an all-enveloping, pixelated immersion, just as Felix Gonzalez-Torres's *Untitled: Portrait of Ross in L.A.* is an ever-depleting mass of candy that begins at a measure equal to his lover's weight.

Both the possibility and reality of his work being viewed in progress disturbed Büchel as well. In an email to Joseph Thompson, he wrote, "How then do you dare with your lack of understanding to install elements and details totally wrong in the show, without my approval, and against my intention. . . . Did you ever realize that your institution and your job is based on art production and that you destroy the condition of its existence, the artwork and the artist concept, by doing this? I guess not, unless [sic] you wouldn't do it."[8]

To show a work in progress or refrain if the artist regards it as incomplete. Here were two choices. At their most reductionist, each outlined the quandary that curatorial intervention embodies. At one extreme is an institution, potentially mediating an artist's work, which emerges for public consumption in some guise. At the other extreme, the artist—who asserts that any intervention will rupture the very essence of the work. Somewhere outside the two, yet absent from either, is the audience—often unaware of negotiations and compromises, immersed in the experience that is its outcome. In fact, it is possible that this audience may have no definable interest in experiencing specific art, as the mere experience of art will often do. Brad Troemel, in the *New Enquiry*, suggests, "the average viewer may be wholly oblivious to what is being addressed, the artists featured, or their stated intentions without some level of *a priori* familiarity with the art world. For this viewer, it's the museum rather than the art that has been sought out, and although artworks are assumed to be inside, any art for them will do."[9] As a result, MASS MoCA is confined by a potentially disinterested, or accidental, spectator, while Büchel is destabilized by the nature of any visually engaged experience.

As a result, in North Adams, Massachusetts, the parties never arrived at a workable compromise. So the matter wound its way through the courts. In September 2007, MASS MoCA received a summary judgment in its favor, which granted the museum legal authority to exhibit *Training Ground* in its partially completed state. A somewhat hollow victory, the ruling would—and did—generate as many ethical and professional conundrums as it resolved. While institutionally, the determination was favorable, conceptually and philosophically the decision provided relief that the museum did not necessarily want to exercise. Fortuitously, any further disagreements relating to the work's display were preempted by Director Thompson's decision to forgo any further exhibition of *Training Ground*. MASS MoCA, favorable ruling in hand, abandoned any additional work related to Büchel's project.

Still, Büchel persisted. He appealed, continuing to assert that his artistic integrity had been compromised and, or even more importantly, so too had his artist's rights. Three years later, the federal court in Boston remarked "[t]hat convergence between artist and artwork does not await the final brushstroke or the placement of the last element in a complex installation."[10] In his opinion, Judge Lipez observed:

> [Büchel] called the Museum disorganized and faulted it for underestimating the scope of his project. He felt that Museum employees, by failing to precisely carry out his detailed instructions and making artistic decisions in his stead, had generated even more work for his crew, as numerous components of the installation had to be reworked to Büchel's specifications. In general, he felt that the Museum was trying to scale back his artistic vision without consulting him.[11]

Both Judge Ponsor at first instance and Judge Lipez on appeal explored the issue of intentionality, Ponsor directly, Lipez implicitly. Although each decision hinged on a limited legal question of artists' rights, a larger, subtler clash between intentionality and intervention stirred. Justice Ponsor draws a distinction while equating curatorial and administrative agency, observing that MASS MoCA was "entitled to present" the unfinished installation to the public if it posted a disclaimer that would "inform anyone viewing the exhibit that the materials assembled in Building 5 constitute an unfinished project that [did] not carry out the installation's original intent."[12] Judge Ponsor's ruling demanded an acknowledgment—that the museum make its intervention transparent.

Judge Ponsor's decision is complicated by the fact that MASS MoCA performed several roles. Writing on the controversy, K. E. Gover recalled a conceptual assertion made by art historian and theorist Rosalind Krauss:

> Even as museums become more and more involved in the production of artworks rather than their mere exhibition, they tend to be regarded more as artistic midwives or patrons than co-creators. While there is nothing wrong in principle with this practice, it deliberately disrupts the usual relation between artist and institution. As a result it can leave both in a peculiarly vulnerable position for which there is little legal or theoretical precedent.[13]

As Krauss implies, and Gover reaffirms, the precedent defining the artist–institution relationship falters from the very moment that collaboration emerges. The difficulty lies in how the partnership is defined. Is it (as is commonly termed) a collaboration, or instead does the institution merely provide personnel that should implement the artist's plans? Gover chronicles MASS MoCA's multifarious roles: the artist's assistant and his benefactor and a public institution. More colloquially, these are helper, patron, and presenter. While none of these roles definitively contradict, they are structured from the outset to impact different museum units and to achieve specific goals. In *Training Ground,* for example, the question of financial support—often the responsibility of a museum's development department—is discussed often.[14] These relationships operate much as pure economies of supply and demand might: one may provide limitless assistance and limited funds, but it is unlikely (if not inconceivable) that an institution could offer limitless assistance and limitless funds—a logical fallacy where endless opportunity and boundless resources could potentially lead to a priceless artwork. While the museum offered infrastructure, resources, and skill, it had to do so within limits.

Regardless, authorship and intentionality would eventually supersede schedules or economies. On appeal, Judge Lipez made three transformational observations: one, that intentionality (including artistic vision and detailed instruction) is established contemporaneously with the conceptualization of a work;[15] two, that any creative decisions made by individuals other than the artist are problematic (one might argue here whether such decisions are rightfully called "artistic");[16] and three, that alterations to the realization of an artist's vision should require consultation or dialogue.[17] His factual summary reinforced the legal determination that Büchel should have retained, in perpetuity, both the authorship of and the agency for *Training Ground for Democracy*. The museum responded to Judge Lipez's decision, stating "we are confident that we exercised appropriate curatorial care and diligence in our handling of the work in progress."[18]

"Appropriate curatorial care and diligence." Büchel's disputes with MASS MoCA did not predominantly center upon either, although both were raised explicitly or implicitly. The central issues were institutional capacity—could MASS MoCA deliver his vision—and artistic versus curatorial or institutional determination (i.e., the operation of divergent agencies that would by necessity produce differing results). For Büchel, intentionality and agency, vision and production, were irrevocably intertwined—such is the nature of creative agency itself. That MASS MoCA would assert a construction of "appropriate curatorial care and diligence" did little to address Büchel's concerns. From Büchel's perspective, his critique of perceived shortcomings were questions of type, meaning who was doing what with the installation as well as the matter of degree—was the work being realized to his specified standards. From the instant MASS MoCA proceeded in any direction—altering, engaging with, or furthering Büchel's work; unveiling, temporarily revealing, obscuring, or publicizing the work in progress—*Training Ground* became mediated, existing outside Büchel's intentionality (regardless of how infinitesimally) and tipping into the problematics of intervention.

Yet, for viewers (who ultimately created the conditions for Büchel's rights to be asserted, subsumed, and in this case, determined by the appeals court to have been violated), any nuanced shift from "artist as creator" to "institution as creator" may well have been imperceptible, or even irrelevant. The phenomenological subjectivity of viewing is intertwined with the process of reception. The impact of the experiential occurs to demolish both anticipation and imagination. As conflicts surrounding *Training Ground* became public, arts-interested viewers and readers began to follow every development closely—up to and including the multiyear legal proceedings. And, while Büchel appears to have had both the means and motivation to assert his rights, and to respond, not every artist would be in a similar position. And, should they find themselves in similar circumstances, what—and how might they—define this experience?

Is *this* what the phrase *curatorial intervention* means? Does it identify an event—think an exhibition—and, if so, does it require proactivity? Or is curatorial intervention a chronicle—an ex post facto analysis? Perhaps, curatorial intervention is a quality, like creative expression. Or is curatorial intervention a state of experience, oscillating and defining the potentialities of change?

A concrete definition is elusive, though in operation the implications of curatorial intervention are more readily observed. At its core, curatorial intervention means mediation, the agency of a disparate power relationship altering the experience of an artwork between the artist and the work's audience. At times, curatorial intervention is a minute deflection; at others, an unstoppable force. Curatorial intervention is animated through change, alteration, reconstruction, reinterpretation. Curatorial intervention is—to borrow from Friedrich Nietzsche—a revaluation that remains opaque: "All the sciences have now to pave the way for the future task of the philosopher; this task being understood to mean, that he must solve the problem of value, that he has to fix the hierarchy of values."[19] The recognition and definition of curatorial intervention is, too, a "preparing the way." Identifying and defining curatorial intervention means making opacity transparent and resubstantiating the invisible hand of economics. Except curatorial intervention alters perception and experience rather than supply and demand. It may well move the market, but first, it moves the (ready)made.

Today, the term *intervention* is fraught and loaded. Radical actions that could mitigate health concerns are termed interventions; to interfere with an outcome is an intervention. But intervention can also operate with opacity. According to Merriam-Webster, an intervention may "occur or lie between two things." Here lies the most problematic issue with the definition: curatorial intervention is not the space that exists between two things. Historically, the two subjects that define any extant gap between artwork and experience are artist and viewer, intender and receiver. This bilateral interrelation for art is prevalent. Artists make, audiences see. But this simplified framework has never truly operated. Instead, curators and institutions have filled the void, deflecting and reorienting the experience of works of art. Whether individual or institutional, this deflecting is made manifest through the operation of curatorial intervention. In what follows, intervention is not by necessity a negative occurrence. At times, the most radical changes are driven by an almost imperceptible impetus. Again, I think here of Nietzsche, in his introduction to *Twilight of the Idols*, speaking of "eternal idols that are here touched with a hammer as if with a tuning fork."[20] It is time to see if the dialectical rhetoric that binds artist and audience rings true, or if curatorial intervention is the unseen and almost imperceptible hammer that strikes to determine the true tones of intervention and reception.

Mapping curatorial intervention means following a syncretic thread that leads neither to artist nor audience. Instead, its well-worn yet seldom-seen path leads toward a space where "curators as constructors" is synonymous with "curators as authors." If a history of postmodern exhibitions is defined, in part, by a creative–curatorial schism, then the moment of intervention also stands as the historical moment of mediated meaning construction.

Imagine the mood at Robert Morris's desk, or kitchen table, or bar as he pens his response to Harald Szeemann's curatorial framework for *documenta 5*—the original creative clash with the interventionists. Szeemann, identified as the "general secretary" for the exhibition—and today remembered as the exhibition's sole curator, despite the participation of many collaborators in various roles, including Bazon Brock and Jean-

Christophe Amman—"laid the basis for independent art curating to create its own professional space within the art world: to become a sub-discourse within the broader art discourse, as well as a distinct profession with its own institutions (e.g. training, residencies) and a job market."[21] Here is Szeemann's initial curatorial framework from his *First Exhibition Concepts for documenta 5*:

> For some time already exhibition directors generally have been tending to replace formal principles that have been adhered to up to now by those of content. The *thematic exhibition* is a result of these reflections. The whole of the material shown in an exhibition is determined by a thematic context, which a) is derived from existing work, or b) is formulated independently of already existing material.[22]

Szeemann goes on to further outline that the theme will be driven both by "the existing work of individual artists or groups and from the present state of thought about general social problems."[23] As a theme, it was indicative of its time. As an indication of the aesthetic and creative intentions of the artists invited to participate, not so much. As a result, Morris and 10 of his contemporaries regarded Szeemann to have overstepped his curatorial bounds during his construction of the exhibition. The artists penned a collective missive to Szeemann, to which Morris offered a scathing single-page supplement:

> I do not wish to have my work used to illustrate misguided sociological principles or outmoded art-historical categories. I do not wish to participate in international exhibitions which do not consult with me as to what work I might want to show but instead dictate to me what will be shown. I do not wish to be associated with an exhibition which refuses to communicate with me after I have indicated my desire to present work other than that which has been designated. Finally, I condemn the showing of my work which has been borrowed from collectors without my having been advised.[24]

In this now-famous letter, Morris outlined the limits he perceived Szeemann's new, *interventionist* approach to exceed: consultation, communication, representation. Morris asserted a creative right to determine which of his works—if any—should be included in *documenta 5*, or for that matter, in any exhibition. He demanded the opportunity to disassociate himself from exhibitions that thwarted or misrepresented his artistic visions and specifications. And he critiqued curators who borrowed existing works, rather than collaborating directly with artists to produce exhibition-specific objects, concepts, and projects.

For *documenta 5*, Morris also shared his many concerns about artworks—unmoored from intentionality—being used variously to illustrate widely divergent principles or perceptions; they could materialize without consultation and minus the artist's knowledge or approval or be works an artist had disavowed or artworks that appeared detached from any specific intention in contradiction to the artist's position regarding the curatorial concept or theme. In his correspondence, Morris goes so far as to suggest that Szeemann has infringed upon his creative rights by exhibiting work "which has been borrowed from collectors without my having been advised."

Of course, Szeemann and his collaborators, in fact, had multiple concepts for the exhibition. The second situated their interventionist tendencies even more directly, as Szeemann, Brock, and Amman offered an additional framework—titled "Second Concept for *documenta 5*," where the three asserted:

> Since the stimulating of the reception of the event and experience-character can only be one—if important—precondition for proper reception of the theme, there is an absolute need for a smaller second exhibition in addition to the central exhibition, where the accent lies unequivocally on categories other than those of event and experience. In this second exhibition the public should above all be offered the cognitive, psychomotor, and socio-emotional conditions for adequate reception of the theme. This exhibition within the exhibition is *The Visitors' School* of *documenta 5*.[25]

This missive could just as well be titled "The Curatorial Interventionists' Manifesto." For what it does, and what it asserts, is directly motivated by a curatorially driven desire to shift audiences' experiences toward those that may feel unfamiliar or disconcerting. In their words, their goal is to construct experiences for audiences using means "which do not enjoy excessive popularity among regular art exhibition visitors."[26] One must wonder what could have compelled Szeemann, Brock, and Amman to position themselves at the periphery of classical aesthetic experience while they were centering themselves at the apex of curatorial intervention in the artist-audience exchange? This is the theoretical genesis of what follows.

Given Szeemann's expanded curatorial role—and, according to Dorothee Richter, the photographic evidence that mirrors this new curator/artist/audience hierarchy[27]—any model of curatorial practice that aligned with his vision would have been deemed interventionist. By necessity, Szeemann's *documenta 5* concepts would have to—at least occasionally—utilize artists' works differentially to construct specific curatorial narratives, and the corollary anticipated cultural dialogues—concerns Morris foreshadowed. In fact, *documenta 5* may have merely catalyzed the most fully formed manifestation of the principles and practices Szeemann had been developing at least since his appointment as director of the Kunsthalle Bern and, perhaps, as early as 1957. By 1972, Szeemann's examinations and interpretations of curatorial practice were established, and his concepts for alternative curatorial frameworks were well formed. What seems at first glance like a radical shift in practice is the outcome of a decade and a half of developing, defining, asserting, and refining his construction of the curator's role. His curatorial practice had been informed by two of its most distinctive European practitioners: George Schmidt, at the Kunsthalle Basel, and William Sandberg, director of the Stedelijk Museum until 1963. Of Sandberg's practice, Szeemann remarked:

> Sandberg was obsessed with information. Sometimes he exhibited only part of a diptych, for instance, or left a good work out of the show altogether because it was reproduced in the catalogue. For him ideas and information counted more than the experience of the object.[28]
>
> In a sense, I combined both approaches in my shows to achieve what I like to think of as selective information and/or informative selection. This is how I view my Kunsthalle years. In putting together an exhibition, I took both connoisseurship and the dissemination of pure information into account and transformed both. That's the foundation of my work.[29]

To some extent, Szeemann's curatorial appropriation of works by Morris and others served to recontextualize each as a conceptually empty vessel. I am reminded of the "nothing" that is Heidegger's nihilation of the very being of an object. If one were to consider various degrees of intervention, the action of nihilation—that curatorial intervention *ne plus ultra*—would in its absolute agency transform an artwork from "the work," grounded in specificity, to "a work," adrift, subjectively and conceptually separate from the context in which it was grounded. The propensity to see a cleaving between artist and curator creates conditions where curators may decontextualize or recontextualize works. But, as Liz Wells notes, there is very little long-term value in proceeding in this way. In her words, "Exhibitions wherein a curator has determined a theme or proposition, or used the work of others merely to illustrate it and produce writing geared towards anchoring and constraining interpretative potential, rarely hold interest for very long."[30]

Just as nihilation subsumes context to object, Szeemann's then-new, interventionist model situated curatorial agency beyond intention in ways that, conceptually, could be seen to be anchored in the intentionality Wells describes above and viewed through the lens of Sartrean bad faith. This new power dynamic did not go unnoticed. Daniel Buren, omitted from Szeemann's earlier *Live in Your Head: When Attitudes Become Form*, became a chameleonic participant at *documenta 5*—invited, but determined to undermine Szeemann's curatorial interventions. Buren went so far as to describe Szeemann's profession as one in which "curators were becoming superartists who used artworks like so many brushstrokes in a huge painting."[31] True, Szeemann's—and, today, any other curator's—exhibition narrative could transform meaning wholly independent from an artist's intention. In such a moment, the physicality of the artwork—its objectness—would become detached, hollowed of meaning. Today, the curatorial agency that Morris rebelled against occurs far more frequently than one might expect. At times, less overtly; at others, with a greater degree of self-reflection. Just over 30 years after *documenta 5*, Ivan Gaskell, speaking at the symposium *How Museums Do Things with Artworks*, remarked:

> When discussing display we may disagree among ourselves about the specific use of any given artwork on a particular occasion, even to the extent of believing that its maker's intentions are being betrayed, but the multivalency of artworks, and the temporary nature of any such display, should allay any fears that irreparable harm is being done.[32]

Multivalent artworks, temporary displays, and believing that its maker's intentions are being betrayed . . . this sounds surprisingly familiar—a contemporary reimagination of Szeemann's "Second Concept for *documenta 5*." And, while Szeemann sought to deflect his agency through references to unfamiliar and unpopular museumgoing experiences, Gaskell instead hints at the temporary nature of displacement and seeks to allay fears.

But what of intention? Why should creativity subjectivity ground experiential interpretation? A concise overview of the trajectory of intention is chronicled in Charles Palermo's *Intention and Interpretation*, a special issue of nonsite.org. In the introduction, Palermo outlines a new potential for a return to intentionality—an assertion that, despite postmodernism's assertions to the contrary, the mere existence of subjective interpretation did not negate intentionality. Palermo writes, "Debates about intention don't just affect how we talk and write about art; they affect in a very common and direct way the practices by which art is made."[33] Palermo, writing about how intentionalist interpretation and analysis have, effectively, been displaced remarks, "One now routinely reads rote refusals of intentional interpretation and insouciant claims for the spectator's prerogative in making meaning. Such refusals and claims may be right—that's a question we may discuss today—but their reexamination, which is to say this conversation, is overdue."[34]

A theme is beginning to emerge: one could suggest that, within a totalizing framework of interventionist reinterpretation, meanings of works are not only unstable but malleable, just as the ways they might be experienced are manipulated. The constant within each new exhibition framework? Curators—each offering myriads of surprising rationales for positioning artworks outside an artist's intentions. If, previously, the somber frame of the exhibition had been systemically and systematically undermined by the artist (think Duchamp's *Sixteen Miles of String* and *1200 Bags of Coal*) from the late 1960s, even those most aggressive attacks on the institution—Beuys's *Fattecke* (literally, made from fat), Richard Serra's *Splash* pieces, or Michael Heizer demolishing the forecourt of the

Kunsthalle Bern with a wrecking ball for his *Bern Depression*—were as constrained by the exhibition's curatorial framework as they were by the institution's physical architecture. Interpretationally or intentionally, one could consider Beuys's *Fattecke* and Serra's *Splash* works precisely for their aggressive colonization of an institutional architectural limit—the base, the angle, that site where wall meets floor.

Regardless, *documenta 5* becomes a harbinger for the curatorial interventions to come. The emergent interventionist structure may well careen between evident and inferred, between celebrated and subdued, but, from this moment forward, the artist–audience dialectical exchange is essentially dead. And while there may be some need for its resuscitation, institutions have been content to stand on the periphery, if not to allow intention to pass completely by.

This scenario underscores both the theoretical and practical issues at play concerning curatorial intervention. First, it is imperative to differentiate between curatorial intervention and curatorial activism as defined by Maura Reilly in her book of the same name. As Reilly outlines, curatorial activism is, in principle, an oppositionist frame to curatorial intervention. It may be plausible to argue that curatorial activism is the positive construct of curatorial intervention, and, to some extent, that seems viable. Reilly situates many well-known curators within the curatorial activism frame—"Jean Hubert Martin, [the now late] Okwui Enwezor, Rosa Martinez, Jonathan Katz, Camille Morineau, Michiko Kasahara, Paweł Leszkowicz, Juan Vicente Aliaga, Connie Butler, Simon Njami, Amelia Jones, among others."[35] Yet activism operates at a different frequency than interventionism. Reilly's definition of activism situates curatorial practice as an equalizing strategy designed to give voice to discourses and artists traditionally marginalized within institutional frames, and to address and redress "structural/systemic" issues that have long plagued exhibitions.

Where curatorial intervention and curatorial activism differ is in their foundational construct. Curatorial intervention is, as I perceive it, opaque, and transactional; curatorial activism is transparent, and situational. As Reilly explains, her goal in *Curatorial Activism* is to "think about gender, race, and sexuality." For each of the exhibitions Reilly examines in *Curatorial Activism*, there is a clear thematic that can be evaluated to determine the depth and effectiveness of the curatorial outcomes. Curatorial activism is holistic; curatorial intervention is, primarily, individualistic. Curatorial activism is, in Reilly's words, revisionist, which would mean it is also constructivist. Curatorial intervention is *also* revisionist—yet internalist.[36]

Interventionalism as internalism can manifest through either individual or institutional perceptions that a specific construction or manifestation of a work is correct—leading to further interrogations regarding questions of completion, as was illustrated in the Christoph Büchel analysis above. Whenever an institution decides to interpret an artist's vision, the result is mediated. The shift from artist as creator to curator or institution as creator should reasonably be expected to be transparent. Instead, this notion of transparency is merely entrenched in popular culture. Anton Vidokle writes in 2010 of having recently participated in a conference on curatorial practice in which the press release described the "figure of the curator as a knowledgeable and transparent agent."[37] Curatorial transparency is an aspirational principle lauded by the late Okwui Enwezor at a curatorial practice conference in the late 1990s, sharing, "part of the responsibility of the curators is to say, 'This is what I am doing, and I am not the final word.'"[38] Knowledgeable, indeed. To facilitate interventionalist transparency, Vidokle outlines four key factors that define relationships between curators and artists: overreaching, the job, curator as producer, and artist as curator.[39]

Overreaching involves the tendency by curators to situate alternative practitioners within the framework of art—his example, a chef who uses food "as" art, rather than an artist like Rikrit Tiravanija who creates art through food. *The job* is a reference to a perceived shift in agency—from the critic to the curator—that consolidates institutional and expressive power within a single individual. *Curator as producer* is perhaps the most problematic and germane construct for our purposes. He asks, "How do you exactly say no to the curator who invited you to participate in a show, but seems to want to credit herself as a collaborator or co-author, when you risk not being invited the next time?"[40]

Substitute "institution as producer" for "artist as curator," and one must wonder whether Büchel's rights under the Visual Artists Rights Act of 1990 would have been violated if work on *Training Ground for Democracy* had continued, but the installation had been dismantled before *ever* being exhibited. It may be possible to infer that, during the Büchel–museum schism, ongoing publicity meant that the specific shift from "artist-as-creator" to "institution-as-creator" was known to anyone who experienced the piece—but this is not necessarily the case. So where does the responsibility for transparency regarding curatorial or institutional intervention lie?

None of this would be problematic if not for a more complex set of circumstances that construct the experience of a work of art. These circumstances structure the artist-audience exchange and mediate one's experiences of a work of art. What follows begins with a single observation that grounds the project's theoretical framework, that reception theory, appropriated in its entirety from literature—then overlaid wholesale onto the visual arts—cannot (and does not) adequately account for the role of the curator. This problem becomes apparent particularly and specifically when addressing the conundrum of the artist-audience exchange and audiences' experiences of works of art. The problem arises, in part, since reception theory deals predominantly with experiencing literary works; overlaying it onto the visual arts is structurally flawed from the outset.

The issue is complicated by questions concerning how curatorial agency and power first emerge within what is classically regarded as a dualistic, possibly dialectic exchange. The existence or absence of curatorial agency grounds and positions how this established structure is altered. The question derives, in part, from an interrogation of whether curatorial agency is implied, meaning that there is an expectation of its existence or whether it is positioned as a supplement to the traditional artist-audience exchange.

The ways in which curatorial practice and, by extension, the notion of curatorial intervention, might mediate the structural and metaphorical relationships between both author and viewer, and artist and audience, are not new. One might refer here to curator, writer, and educator Robert Storr, speaking at the Curating Now: Imaginative Practice/Public Responsibility conference in 2000:

> I do think curators have a medium, and if they retain some humility and master their craft, their relation to that medium and to art itself is like that of a good editor to a good novelist. Although it's not the same thing as being a novelist, being an editor involves a deep identification with a living aesthetic. That aesthetic vantage point is as important or, in many respects, more important than what we usually call "ideas" about art. As a curator, you can work through problems by working with materials and working with artists who are working with materials, instead of always approaching things as if a curator was primarily an explainer or educator.[41]

As an editor to a novelist—were it only that simple. The logical flaw, so the theoretical paradigm posits, is that reception theory—modally dual and structurally binary—cannot (and does not) address the fact that, in mediating the visual arts exchange, the curator (and their agency) shifts from collaborative to imperative. Quite simply, it shifts from the "you could . . ." to the "could you . . .?" And, in doing so, not only does the potential for curatorial intervention appear, but it also first appears to potentially rupture the binary nature of reception theory itself. Obviously, if true, this would be problematic. So, alternatively, classical reception theory in the visual arts presents the curator as absent. The problem Storr raises is discussed by Rossen Ventzislavov and Sue Spaid, over several issues of the *Journal of Aesthetics and Art Criticism*, in one of the few extended theoretical and philosophical exchanges on the potential operations of curatorial intervention. Briefly, Ventzislavov argues for a construction of curatorial practice (and thereby curatorial intervention) in which curators are viewed as creative practitioners, just like artists.[42] Spaid disagrees, arguing that the cognitive value added by curators is not equal to the aesthetic value created by artists.[43] Ventzislavov replies, suggesting that he sees few areas of disagreement between their positions and that, in fact, curators provide artists with a benefit through recognizing the interpretative extensions that curatorial intervention may provide.[44]

Perhaps the reason for the apparent absence of the curator is that they are, in fact, a specter. Or, if not curators themselves, their agency is spectral, at least to the extent that by its action there is intervention. One might think here of the famous dictum of Karl Marx and Friedrich Engels that opens the *Communist Manifesto* (1848), which would be applicable were it slightly revised: *There is a specter haunting curating, and that specter is intervention.*

And, as is implied above, the act of curatorial intervention—should it exist—would be the foundational differentiation and the primary rupture that distinguishes curators from artists. This would potentially even situate intervention as a necessary function of curatorial practice.

To find a site where reception can be located or situated, one must tease out threads within other source materials. Which nexus will be the *point de capiton*, the quilting point, the moment Jacques Lacan defines as one in which the constant slippages between signifier and signified are temporarily halted.[45] For our purposes, that quilting point is the curator, and the structure being interrogated is artist–curator–audience, rather than the more traditional artist–object–audience. If this alternative structure is applied, then theorists such as Brian O'Doherty, writing in his essay "Content as Context," can observe that the artist–audience relationship tests both the social and structural orders and is absorbed by social institutions.[46] By extension, one may argue that the site of this absorption is the museum and the sponge is the curator. As Robert Storr remarks:

> Curatorial practice's area of competence is, first and foremost, art. When curators lose sight of this fact, and of art itself—no matter how critical any particular body of work may be for one or another aesthetic tradition or even for the idea of art—they almost invariably end up doing art and the public a serious disservice.[47]

Even with art at his curatorial center, critics have suggested that Storr's approach can, at times, be "a measured, decorous, highly controlled, somewhat antiseptic, strangely straight-jacketed affair."[48] This is Jerry Saltz, at Artnet.com, critiquing the ways in which curatorial practice, particularly in the United States, makes its alchemy manifest with varying degrees of success. In the same essay, which reviews the *2007 Venice Biennale, documenta,* and *Sculpture Projects Münster*, Saltz pivots to an entirely different perspective. Whereas before, Storr's curatorial narrative was found to be "somewhat antiseptic," Saltz criticizes Münster because the organizers Brigitte Franzen and Kaspar König haven't curated enough:

> Nothing really holds this show together. There's no real idea or polemic behind it—no point of view about public art, the current moment, sculpture in general, Germany, Europe, or whatever. It's just a bunch of artists who the curators like.[49]

Where intervention does emerge consistently is within recent analyses of nontraditional or noninstitutional frameworks and in models or experiences that focus on independent curatorial practice. Nancy de Freitas, in her essay "Breathing Space for Experience," observes that interventions commonly occur within structures with a strong educational component, remarking that "other interventions, crossing over the art/curatorship/education boundaries, have also contributed to the exploration and critique of curating as a contemporary practice in different cultural contexts."[50] De Freitas cites the SUMMIT Initiative, the Resistance Art Festival, and The Go-Between as community or educationally based projects that intervened precisely at the points of community engagement rather than within the confines of the traditional art institution.[51]

The idea of curatorial intervention also briefly appears in discussions surrounding conservation and sustainability in artworks. In his 1983 essay, "Impermanence: A Curator's Viewpoint," Peter Cannon-Brookes asks, "[c]an, in fact, the efforts of the curator be construed as deliberately distorting the artistic intentions of the creator of the work of art? And thus do they constitute an unjustifiable intervention?"[52] Cannon-Brookes pinpoints two key questions that do not appear to have been pursued further. One, are there instances in which curatorial actions truly do distort artistic intentions? If so, how should institutions and audiences address this potential, or its occurrence? Two, how would these curatorial interventions be considered? Would there be situations in which they would seem justifiable? Not only does Cannon-Brookes question the action, but he also raises the ethical issues inherent therein. By dealing specifically with issues of impermanence, he is able to make distinctions: where artists knowingly make qualities such as entropy key components of their works, they should be left alone; where the instability is the result of a lack of knowledge, curators and institutions should be able to intervene—potentially prior to the work being realized.[53]

And what of the instances in which the curator invites the artist to engage with both the audience and the institution and then decides that the engagement should be mediated prior to being actualized? One need only recall artist Andrea Fraser speaking of her experience in the 1993 Whitney Biennial. After a series of failed proposals for her project, the institution approved one that involved interviewing museum staff for the creation of an audio "guide." Fraser explains, "I wanted to represent the same issues that the curators were trying to address in the Biennial, but in terms of their own interactions and the conflicts within the museum, and to communicate those issues directly by constructing the tape so that they would be enacted in it. And although I knew that that wasn't the way they would want me to engage those issues, I still felt that I did it in good faith."[54] In the end, the museum became nervous about Fraser's tape and its contents; the project became compromised because of museum demands regarding final approval—including script oversight and audiotape editing.[55]

There is no clearer way to grasp these expectations than to imagine these complaints applied to an installation or to an artist-curated exhibition. Although both curating and installation are concerned with selection, they function within different discursive spheres: curatorial selection is always an ethical negotiation of preexisting authorships, rather than the artistic creation of meaning *sui generis*.[56]

Still, both Szeemann's and Gaskell's curatorial contextualizations and—as Terry Smith outlines, a corroborating interpretation—have the potential to operate distinct from intervention. To do so, curatorial practice must function at the point where the artist–audience and intention–reception exchanges remain intact. Curatorial thinking transforms into curatorial intervention and is made manifest to the audience only when its agency becomes visible and available. As Terry Smith notes in his *Thinking Contemporary Curating*:

> Within the space of the exhibition itself, the curator's interpretation remains unstated, implicit. In its explicit form, it usually becomes available to the viewer later—in the catalogue, for example—as a supplement to the understanding that he or she arrived at while taking in the exhibition.[57]

The transformation of the art encounter into two experiences problematizes the comprehension of intervention. In reading Terry Smith, viewers, as readers, encounter two proximate experiences, interrelated yet distinct from one another. There is the visual-physical proximate experience of viewing, which establishes the viewer-artist relationship, and subsequent, as well as the visual-narrative proximate experience of language. The curator's agency must oscillate between the two. The agency is implicit experientially—as the viewer physically encounters the work, and, explicit, theoretically and linguistically, as the viewer transforms into reader and examines the curator's narrative exposition. In such an instance, where would curatorial interventionality "attach" to the artwork—the physical or the expository experience—since both are proximate?

You can stand on top of it. Incredible. Slip on a pair of Tyvek booties, and you are in a studio in Springs, New York, wondering if you can figure out exactly where *Lavender Mist*, or *Autumn Rhythm*, or maybe even *Blue Poles* might have been laid out on the floor. The plywood sheathing that skins the floor of the studio is not a work, but it is of the work. It is, both literally and figuratively (for once), the ground, the foundational support, physically and conceptually, for that radical form of expression that emerges as gestural abstraction. So remember the booties and the floor as you consider what Valerie Casey's "Staging Meaning: Performance in the Modern Museum" reveals:

> As the contemporary museum has sought to appeal to its experience-oriented audience, the centrality of curatorial intervention has increased, and the processes of display used to convey information are often privileged over the particularity of objects. This strategy of stage-setting is expressed quite literally in the physical installation of artworks—even the ordinarily purist MoMA employed extraordinary display techniques in the Jackson Pollock 1998–99 exhibition. . . . Scrubbed free of the paint spills and splotched surfaces in the actual studio, the sterilized diorama at MoMA was reinterpreted and reinscribed as a different kind of sacred space, one which conformed to the ordered voice of its curatorial intermediaries.[58]

Scrubbed free of every gesture that brings Pollock's and Krasner's Springs, New York, space to life, MoMA's simulacral studio becomes artwashed. Absent were not only the traces and gestures that Pollock and Krasner had inscribed across the studio floor, but also every physical reference to Pollock's hypermasculinity and narcissism. This lack, just through the singular decision to omit the studio floor. Casey is spot on: the studio floor's blotches, drips, and stains are both literal markers and psychological referents to Pollock's flawed character, and, in scrubbing them from the museum, MoMA primed Pollock for a more monochrome history—and furthered revision and rehabilitation of Pollock's creative and personal reputations.

If, for Pollock, the studio was his site of creative immersion, for viewers a museum or gallery should be a site to experience some similar perception. And, just as the construction of Pollock's legend hinged upon his regular and repeated exchanges with a very specific, arts-informed audience—Pollock and Namuth, Pollock and Guggenheim, Pollock and Parsons—in every instance, the mythos grew from his ability to direct, if not control, the narrative. In 1949, he is static on the pages of *Life* magazine; two years later, he is the creative maverick from Wyoming, a wild aesthetic animal pacing around a wooden deck set against a broad expanse of what looks like marsh grass, cigarette in hand—and those paint-splattered boots, as if through Namuth's jump cuts they might become the allegorical sole of modernist painting.

If we step back for a moment, it is important to remember that inserting curators into the artist–audience exchange remains a radical notion. Apart from attributing authorship to curators—something that is decidedly not the intention of this work—a framework for an artist–curator–audience relationship that is transparent and nonhierarchical has remained elusive. As a result, in those moments when authorship or exhibition-making is not being considered, alternative interpretivist approaches have often involved constructing frames already beyond questions of curatorial intervention, authorship, and mediation. Interventionism has somehow been dispelled from critical or constructive consideration without ever having been fully situated. Consider Paul O'Neill, Mick Wilson, and Lucy Steeds's introduction to *The Curatorial Conundrum: What to Research? What to Study? What to Practice*:

> While in the 1990s the role of the curator was discussed largely through the gloss of the "exhibition-maker," and the expansion of the curatorial role since that time may be understood as the overcoming of the authorial function of the curator, the problematization of the exhibitionary complex—and particularly the development of exhibition-making—has arguably given rise to a less dichotomous construal of the exhibitionary and the curatorial. A notable point of interchange emerges around thinking through exhibition-making, and the interrogation of curatorial knowledges—made manifest in the increased profile given to questions of curatorial labor or exhibition-making when this work is broadly understood, for instance, as actions of practical inquiry congruent with, but not reducible to, other modes of scholarship and experimental research.[59]

Functionally, the interventional obscures the curatorial more than the exhibitionary opposes the authorial. Rather problematically, the ongoing triad of curatorial transparency, agency, and power remains unaddressed. Instead, deeming it simpler to substitute roles for actions, the question disappears. Its absence is enabled partly because neither artists nor audiences are particularly concerned with who is a participant in constructing experiences of art. Theoretically, at least, and presumably practically, it appears to make very little difference to either if the other, or anyone else, is involved in their individual encounter. To push the analogy a little further, consider Alex Farquharson, who asserts that there is a possibility that what matters is not either the artist–audience or artist–curator–audience exchange, but instead who ultimately is responsible for completing the work. According to Farquharson:

> The aversion to so-called "finished" art works, whether they be finished on site or in the studio, often betrays a rather naive and overliteral interpretation of the death of the author—birth of the reader maxim derived from Roland Barthes. All works of art, especially good ones, are open systems that the recipient reformulates in his or her own way at the point of reception. A supposedly finished work will be reformulated as often as a so-called relational or unfinished one. Nicolas Bourriaud quotes Jean-Luc Godard saying as much: "If a viewer says, 'the film I saw was bad,' I say, 'it's your fault; what did you do so that the dialogue would be good?'"[60]

But what if the curator responds, "I wrote the dialogue," meaning that they constructed the narrative that the audience experiences outside the frame of the artwork's intentions. This would be the sine qua non—the without which not—of curatorial intervention. In this moment, the agency of curatorial intervention would become most evident. *Training Ground for Democracy* stands as an example of an artwork that could have devolved into an "institutional" artwork. Instead, both Joseph Thompson and Nato Thompson determined that exhibiting the work publicly outside the desires and preferences of the audience would have significant—and unintended—results. While a select few museum professionals may have seen the work partially completed, *Training Ground for Democracy* remained anchored within Büchel's conceptual framework even when MASS MoCA received a legally determined entitlement to proceed.

The action or experience of reception is not in doubt; works are received when and because they are experienced. But, as Kasper König outlines, even the distinctions between participants within the production–mediation–consumption processes are blurred:

> The artist is also an observer of himself or herself. You can't clearly anticipate or participate between reception and production. The criteria for understanding are quite often being offered along with the work. It's a very dialectical relationship between the maker, the viewer, the museum, or the places where you expect.[61]

The objective here is to understand the shift that occurs along the intention–reception continuum. Paul O'Neill alludes to this framework in *The Culture of Curating and the Curating of Culture(s)*. There, he hypothesizes a model within which curatorial operations and decisions by necessity affect every limit of a work: its literal and physical boundaries, the scope and proper attribution of its authorship, and any mediations it may be subject to, both curatorially and institutionally, before being experienced by an audience. As he explains, in one of Lucy Lippard's late-1960s curatorial projects, her involvement was so substantial—and her prior artistic practice so well known—that it was difficult to determine if she was engaging with the work as a curator or an artist. This type of indeterminate and, at times, even oscillating relationship serves only to further problematize the issue. Using Lippard's experience as a primary example, O'Neill considers the idea of the "curator as *Ausstellungsmacher*" or "independent exhibition-maker," a person with a more significant role than a traditional curator who is more involved with the overall conception and realization of an exhibition.

> I have always believed that it is the artist who creates a work, but a society that turns it into a work of art, an idea that is already in Duchamp and a lot of other places. In most cases, museums have failed to see the consequences of this notion. I have always considered myself to be a "co-producer" of art. Now, do not misunderstand me. I do not

> mean this in the sense of dictating to an artist: "Listen, now paint the upper left-hand corner red!" but rather in the sense of participating as a museum—as a mediating institution—in the process that transforms a work into a work of art.[62]

The most perplexing question that will operate around curatorial intervention concerns how one defines its occurrence. In this regard, it is valuable to consider the late writings of Martin Heidegger, where he suggests that the experiential is not always defined by its most visible qualities. Instead, Heidegger's notion of inconspicuousness may be vital. As Jason Alvis observes, "A phenomenology of the 'Inconspicuous' is a means of investigating and subsequently experiencing (without 'conceiving') phenomena whose intelligibilities oscillate between both presence and absence."[63] Perhaps curatorial intervention exists within this oscillation, and the phenomena of experience, visible and invisible, intelligible and unintelligible, are its inconspicuous manifestations. This is the very crux of the perceptual element of curatorial intervention—that, in its absence, it operates as a presence. What I mean by this is that, through its seeming invisibility—and, by necessity, the assertion that it should operate precisely opposite—curatorial intervention emerges and disappears. Its operation is visible, but its perception/reception is not. To pursue Heidegger further, Alvis observes that one quality of inconspicuousness is that it calls into question "the pretensions of how consciousness constitutes its world and engages in the 'pure inwardness' of intentionality." Inconspicuousness is not the measure of curatorial intervention, however. A little intervention is intervention all the same. The question becomes one of how significantly even the most minor interventions cause artistic intentionality to deviate during its journey from maker to receiver.

NOTES

1. Micchelli, "Christoph Büchel, *Training Ground for Democracy*."
2. Gover, "Christoph Büchel v. Mass MoCA: A Tilted Arc for the Twenty-First Century," 50.
3. Edgers, "Behind Doors, a World Unseen." Correspondence surrounding this question is also found in the exhibits for *Massachusetts Museum of Contemporary Art Foundation, Inc. v. Christoph Büchel,* Massachusetts District Court Case Number 3:2007cv30089. These documents are obtainable for a fee through Public Access to Court Electronic Records (PACER).
4. Case 3:07-cv-30089-MAP, Document 31-14, Filed 8/31/2007, pp. 2 and 3.
5. Case 3:07-cv-30089-MAP, Document 31-65, Filed 8/31/2007, pp. 2 and 3.
6. Edgers, "Behind Doors, a World Unseen," note 65.
7. Ibid.
8. Case 3:07-cv-30089-MAP, Document 31-68, Filed 8/31/2007, pp. 3 and 4.
9. Troemel, "The Accidental Audience."
10. Kennedy, "Artists Rights Act Applies in Dispute, Court Rules."
11. *Massachusetts Museum of Contemporary Art Foundation Inc. v Büchel,* No. 08-2199, January 27, 2010, FindLaw, https://caselaw.findlaw.com/us-1st-circuit/1500091.html.
12. 593 F.3d 38, *46.

13. Gover, "Christoph Büchel v. Mass MoCA: A Tilted Arc for the Twenty-First Century," 49.

14. Case 3:07-cv-30089-MAP, Document 31-21, Filed 8/31/2007, p. 3 of 6. Case 3:07-cv-30089-MAP, Document 31-51, Filed 8/31/2007, p. 3 of 3. On January 21, 2007, Büchel wrote to Joseph Thompson, "If you are not able to organize the money needed to resume the installation, excluded is any money from Hauser & Wirth and me, as repeatedly mentioned before we started to work on the installation, then we cannot continue."

15. Note 11, above (current chapter).

16. Note 11, above (current chapter).

17. Note 11, above (current chapter).

18. Kennedy, "Artists Rights Act Applies in Dispute, Court Rules."

19. Nietzsche, *On the Genealogy of Morals*, 1:17.

20. Ibid.

21. Fotiadi, "The Canon of the Author."

22. Harald Szeemann, First Exhibition Concepts for Documenta 5, in Szeemann 2008, 95.

23. Ibid.

24. Morris, "Regarding Documenta V."

25. Jean-Christophe Amman, Bazon Brock, and Harald Szeemann, Second Concept for Documenta 5, in Szeemann 2008, 100.

26. Ibid., 102.

27. Dorothee Richter, "On Artistic and Curatorial Authorship," *On Curating* 19 (2013), 45. As Richter explains, "Seen thus, Harald Szeemann's pose is a distinctive positioning, based on historical schemata, especially of the curator as a god/king/man among artists. Comparable to earlier visual demonstrations of power, this picture also endeavours to position its viewers, plainly appealing to their attention. Viewers are thus positioned opposite a scenario in which the artists form a clearly lower-ranking group as the curator's adepts. Szeemann's casual and sprawling pose makes it clear that here is someone who can take liberties. As viewers, we occupy an even lower hierarchical position than the artists; we are situated as eyewitnesses of a spectacle, not as members of a bohemian community. Nevertheless, our role is to provide affirmation."

28. Hans Ulrich Obrist and Harald Szeemann (1996) Curator Interview. Artforum. https://www.artforum.com/print/199609/curator-interview-33047.

29. Ibid.

30. Wells, "Curatorial Strategy as Critical Intervention: The Genesis of Facing East," 31.

31. Hans Ulrich Obrist and Harald Szeemann (1996) Curator Interview. Artforum. https://www.artforum.com/print/199609/curator-interview-33047.

32. Gaskell, "Being True to Artists," 59.

33. Palermo, "Introduction: Intention and Interpretation."

34. Ibid.

35. Reilly, "What Is Curatorial Activism?"

36. Pappas, "Internalist vs. Externalist Conceptions of Epistemic Justification."

37. Vidokle, "Art without Artists."

38. Brenson, "The Curator's Moment," 16.

39. Vidokle, "Art without Artists."

40. Ibid. Vidokle continues, "it seems to me that we should also be very careful to avoid assigning any kind of meta-artistic capacity to curatorial practice. While steps taken in this direction have often been made with good intentions, invoking the expansion of a more general category of 'cultural practice,' they nevertheless carry with them the danger of lending credibility to something like a potential colonization of artistic practice by academia and a new class of cultural managers. If the artist is already expected to question the social, the economic, the cultural, and so forth, then it goes without saying that when a curator supersedes the artist's capacity as a social

critic, we abandon the critical function embodied by the role of the artist and reduce the agency of art."

41. Robert Storr in Paula Marincola and Robert Storr (eds.), (2001). *Curating Now: Imaginative Practice, Public Responsibility*. Philadelphia, PA: Philadelphia Exhibitions Initiative, 9.

42. Rosson Ventzislavov, (2014). "Idle Arts: Reconsidering the Curator." *Journal of Aesthetics and Art Criticism*, 72(1), 84.

43. Sue Spaid, "Revisiting Ventzislavov's Thesis: 'Curating Should Be Understood as a Fine Art'" *The Journal of Aesthetics and Art Criticism* 74, no. 1 (2016): 87–91. Accessed February 7, 2021. http://www.jstor.org/stable/44510217.

44. Rossen Ventzislavov. "The Curator as Artist: Reply to Sue Spaid." *The Journal of Aesthetics and Art Criticism* 74, no. 1 (2016): 91–95. Accessed February 7, 2021. http://www.jstor.org/stable/44510218.

45. Miller, J-A (ed). (1993). *The Seminar of Jacques Lacan, Volume III: The Psychoses, 1955-1956*. New York: W. W. Norton and Company., 258.

46. Brian O'Doherty, (1976. 1986). *Inside the White Cube: The Ideology of the Gallery Space*. Berkeley: University of California Press., 74.

47. Marincola et al., *Pigeons on the Grass Alas*, 50.

48. Saltz, "The Alchemy of Curating."

49. Ibid.

50. De Freitas, "Breathing Space for Experience," 306.

51. Ibid.

52. Cannon-Brookes, "Impermanence: A Curator's Viewpoint," 34.

53. Ibid., 34–35.

54. Blazwick et al., "Serving Audiences," 135.

55. Ibid., 135–36.

56. Bishop, "What Is a Curator?," section 3.

57. Smith, Terry. (2012). *Thinking Contemporary Curating*. New York, NY: Independent Curators International. 45.

58. Casey, "Staging Meaning: Performance in the Modern Museum," 84.

59. O'Neill, Wilson, and Steeds, *The Curatorial Conundrum: What to Study? What to Research? What to Practice?*, 7.

60. Farquharson, "Curator and Artist: The Art of Performative Curating."

61. Thea, *Foci: Interviews with Ten International Curators*, 131.

62. O'Neill, quoted in Hans Ulrich Obrist (2013.) *Ways of Curating*. Zurich: JRP/Ringier, 57.

63. Alvis, "Making Sense of Heidegger's 'Phenomenology of the Inconspicuous' or Inapparent (*Phänomenologie des Unscheinbaren*)," 212.

TWO

Aspects of the Almost Grotesque

Few curators, Harald Szeemann included, have ever truly been able to limit or fully contextualize Daniel Buren's conceptual works. When invited to participate in *documenta 5*, Buren used the opportunity to make a mark on the exhibition itself.[1] Buren, in a candid assessment of the impacts curators have on his works, has said:

> I can do my work, even if the [curator] says something stupid or if he really shows that he did not catch a thing. I do not blame him; I mean, it's his problem. And you never know; even with the simplest things, you never know how people are going to see them.[2]

Still, Ross T. Smith may have been taken aback when he arrived at a gallery exhibiting works from his *Hokianga* series to find the walls painted an unanticipated, and decontextualized, color. First came shock. "They'd painted the walls a sort of mustard yellow," he began. "And I just said, 'Why are the walls this color?'" The color was not the sole issue. Tone and hue were wreaking havoc on Smith's delicately shaded works. "The work is really neutral," Smith explains. "It has soft greys; it's also tea-toned, so the white in the prints is just very creamy and warm." The physical space was certainly having an impact. "The mustard yellow just changes the whole feeling of the work. And," he chided, "it doesn't look right."[3] For whatever reason, his observations fell on deaf ears. "We had words," Smith continued. "They read me the riot act—said that they were the curator, and I had nothing to do with it." Smith paused. "And it was all their choice."[4] That the construct of color would be thwarting the works of an indigenous New Zealand artist—Smith is Māori—seems ironic. Across many of his early series, particularly *Hemi Tuwharerangi Paraha*, and *Hokianga*, Smith often used the subtleties of deep saturation and dark tones to separate his subjects from their surroundings. When the subjects were pushed into the foreground visually, this was often achieved by the addition of high-contrast colors. To see his complex color relationships dulled by an exhibition design decision was deeply problematic—infuriating would not be too strong a word. Oddly enough, Smith's palette shares strong resonances with those of Bill Henson, an Australian photographer whose blues and hues also push his subjects into a soft void. This correlation makes it even more significant that Smith found himself discussing tone. The visual language itself was not absent from similar creative discussions occurring within the region at the time.

Color is one of the choices and interventions curators can and often do make and one of the experiential and perceptual decisions that greatly impact viewers' experiences of art. It was as if Smith were living Daniel Buren's *Four Functions*. At the time, the work was outside the studio, but inscribed within the institution. In *Function of the Studio*, Buren describes how the objectness of an artwork renders it indistinguishable from any other. In that moment, it is not "a Smith" but simply "Smith." In Buren's words, "how it is that, seventy years after being painted, certain canvases by Monet, for example, should be recessed into a salmon-colored wall in a building in Paris, while others in Chicago are encased in enormous frames and juxtaposed with other impressionist works." Culinary references aside, Buren uncovers a key distinction between the creative and the curatorial: considered, yet subjective, constructions of site and space. From Buren's perspective, artists are, and have historically been, disconnected from the decisions made regarding their artworks' reception. When determinations are made in the artist's absence—and, unlike Monet, Smith arrived—those curatorial decisions can be perceived by the artist to be detrimental to both the works and to audiences' experiences of a series. This same observation is made by O'Doherty, who gives William Seitz, then curator at the Museum of Modern Art, credit for "a rare act of curatorial daring."[5]

In certain instances, and within specific curatorial practices, the opportunity to and admission of contextual and conceptual narratives is imperative. Ydessa Hendeles, artist, curator, and philanthropist, describes her curatorial practice as hinging on the opportunity to construct meaning. She explains:

> Herein lies another priority in my practice. To create a visual, experiential journey, each element should be connected to the others and each should enhance the experience of the others. Each work in a show frames the next, contextualizes it and also others, and acts as a counterpoint to elements elsewhere. Meaning and significance mutate and modulate, ultimately growing, as if organically, with alternate and additional layers of meaning accrued.[6]

Within larger institutions in particular, aligning artistic intention with exhibition design decisions can be difficult. Within smaller spaces, this is less often the case. Regardless, the issue at stake is the extent to which the curator's decision impacts how viewers perceive Smith's works, both aesthetically and experientially. And often, curatorial decisions grounded in consultation and experience can have positive impacts on how artists encounter their projects. Were the above a single occurrence, it could well be considered anomalous. But, unsurprisingly, such experiences seem commonplace. The power dynamics that operate within the artist–curator relationship—and which, I would admit, I am guilty of myself—can be recounted with alarming regularity.

One artist (who wishes to remain anonymous) recounted several experiences of curatorial intervention. In the first, they differed with the curator regarding the optimal placement for their work:

> It wasn't so much that they were trying to stop me from what I wanted to do; I could see that—in their mind—they had an idea of the overall shape of the exhibition. Putting my work where I wanted it to go meant it was very dominating. It looked great, but it was very dominating. Maybe that was not their intention. They wanted it to have a lesser place. And that's understandable. That's okay. I'm only one artist, so I can understand that. But apart from those specific instances, I would say that I haven't been pushed around much.

Consider the artist's language for a moment: "dominating," "a lesser place," "I would say that I haven't been pushed around much." These words and phrases allude, possibly subconsciously, to the disparate power relationships that exist between curator and artist.

They continued, narrating another experience—at a different space, working with another curator:

> ARTIST: I'd only seen the gallery once, and it was hard to figure out how this work would go into that space and make sense. In the end, I just said to them, "You're going to have to figure it out, because I'm not here. I can't do it. Just do your best." And then, they did a couple of things that I thought were terrible. They double-hung works that were never supposed to be hung that way. It looked okay, but conceptually it was a travesty as far as I was concerned. But it was done. It was on the wall.
>
> LEVINE: And was there any indication in the exhibition that any of the decisions that had been made about the installation had been made by any member of the exhibitions, curatorial, or administrative teams?
>
> ARTIST: No. You know that doesn't happen.

These experiences, opaque to audiences, directly impacted reception. Historically, the art experience has emphasized the artist–audience exchange, grounded in some manifestation of an audience theory of art, of which, as Nick Zangwill chronicles, there are many:

> According to Monroe Beardsley, a work of art is intentionally endowed with a disposition to produce aesthetic experiences (in an audience). For an expression theory of art, such as Tolstoy's, a work of art expresses emotions and has a disposition to elicit similar emotions (from an audience), or the artist intends that it express and have a disposition to elicit emotions (from an audience). According to Nelson Goodman, a work of art imparts a kind of understanding (to an audience). For Arthur Danto, a work of art makes a "statement" to the artworld (a particular audience). In George Dickie's earlier institutional account, a work of art is deemed by someone to be a candidate for appreciation (by an audience). And in his later account, works of art are intentionally presented to the artworld (a particular audience). According to Jerrold Levinson's historical account, works of art are intended to be regarded (by an audience) in ways similar to the ways that past works of art were regarded (by their audiences). In fact, almost all theories of art that have ever been proposed make some kind of essential reference to an audience.[7]

Zangwill's "Art and Audience" is a meticulous examination of the reasons artists would wish to make art, combined with observations concerning why audiences choose to experience it. The various audience theories of art listed above seek to construct clear linear exchanges from artists, through intention, to audience experience. This linear exchange manifests through a normative relationship between artist and audience. An additional criterion, as Zangwill explains, is that the audience must practice aesthetic evaluation. They must use intellectual differentiation to determine which works have greater or lesser subjective value. With an arts-informed audience, the artist is free to present their work within the experiential space of exhibition. The normative theory of art does not, at least on its surface, create the space for a curator. This dialectical exchange posits a concrete, transactional relationship between the artist and their audience. One might even describe the relationship as interdependent and capable of encompassing these two parties—and only these two.

As a result, the curator is absent. Yet their agency is both omnipresent and insurmountable. Utilizing this power, curatorial practice operates as a supplement to an artist–audience frame, both about and beyond the exchange, simultaneously. Such an experience can operate around the singular object or as the foundation for a larger exchange—whether a solo exhibition, a thematically driven project, or an immediate experience, such as a performance. This transference is found each time curators are observed, or at least critiqued, to have supplanted one context with another. Consider, for example, the Jens Hoffmann–curated *London in Six Easy Steps*, six projects by six curators over a period of six weeks, with each project a single week's duration. While Hoffmann spoke of the project as an examination of the City of London's impacts on contemporary art practices today, critics found the project to abrogate authorial and contextual agency to the participant curators, while at the same time constraining them within the infrastructures the Institute of Contemporary Arts (ICA) had already established. As Paul O'Neill observed, "By giving over the curatorial reins to six guest curators, the ICA declared itself open; but in fact it hid the institutional process involved in selecting these specific six curators at the expense of placing the curatorial responsibility on the invitees. The relatively short duration allocated for each exhibition also put strains on the institution, the invited curators, artists and gallery visitors alike."[8]

By suggesting that there was an implied curatorial hierarchy between institutions, one must conclude that this additional frame set artistic intention, audience experience, and reception at further remove. The notion of a linear, normative relationship between artist and audience should emerge via the artist's capacity to shift the *experiential* site of viewership, regardless of its physical location. Reception should be able to operate virtually, experientially, or psychologically. As Michel Foucault explains in his analysis of *Las Meninas*, Diego Velázquez intellectually interposes viewer with artist:

> The painter is looking, his face turned slightly and his head leaning towards one shoulder. He is staring at a point to which, even though it is invisible, we, the spectators, can easily assign an object, since it is we, ourselves, who are that point: our bodies, our faces, our eyes. The spectacle he is observing is thus doubly invisible: first, because it is not represented within the space of the painting, and, second, because it is situated precisely in that blind point, in that essential hiding-place into which our gaze disappears from ourselves at the moment of our actual looking. (Michel Foucault, *The Order of Things*, 4.)[9]

It occurs, again, as Jacques Lacan explains, through the function of the gaze. In each instance, the formal and conceptual dialectics operate unfettered. Intentionality emerges unmediated from the artist, via the object, to the audience. This is the problem for curatorial practice to the present day. The formal and conceptual dialectics that Foucault references are, he asserts, "the problem for curatorial practice to the present day." But what, precisely, is the problem? In part, it is the realization that for an artist's intentionality to operate, it must in some way engage directly with viewers. As Foucault observes, the doubling capacity of *Las Meninas* is itself twofold: one, and two, the spectator is "without" the painting at the same time they are within—as Velázquez; three, and four, he asserts that the work also operates in "the place into which our gaze disappears from ourselves at the moment of actual looking," making the gaze both experiential and referential. This would be a rupture. One must wonder if the operation of the gaze is contingent upon, or in any way, connected with intentionality, particularly given the transubstantiation of the viewer into the King and Queen of Spain. Does the opportunity, or, more accurately the capacity, to situate oneself within the space of the producer—and their production—exist solely through the operation of this dialectic?

If so, the problematics of curatorial intervention vis-à-vis the artist—and, experienced by the audience—effectively destabilize this blind point to the extent that it would be as if the viewer were experiencing the work by looking over the curator's shoulder.

But this "shoulder" thwarting the viewer's experience is intervention. It is not so much the revelation that each manifestation of curatorial intervention generates its unique implications. Instead, existence supersedes operation. Operation provides the space for specific examination and interpretation: What does it mean to intervene in this way? Why might one intervention be more visible than another? How and when do audiences become aware of these interventions? And are decisions that seem to embody choices determining preference, design, or style as significant as a physical or curatorial intervention that operates specifically to redirect the reception of an artist's work?

Existence, however, remains primary. In both narratives above—Smith's and the anonymous artist's—curatorial agency, with its associated implications, occurred prior to audience experience. This is intervention before reception. One might regard this approach to intervention as being analogous with deflection. The impact on audience experience is dependent upon the extent of the intervention's scope and degree. More substantively, curatorial intervention is the conceptual deflection that destabilizes reception theory, creating that third variable—and an alternative intellectual framework—upon which curators may build.

For any interventionist theory of curatorial practice, the absence of reception theory is crucial. Most often, critical examinations of curatorial practice, its agency and operations, stand as preconditions that exist in a space a priori to exhibition or reception. Since curatorial intervention can operate outside intentionality or reception, however, it operates unidirectionally as a litmus for both the agency of the artist and the experience of the audience.

In 2015, Bayeté Ross Smith, a Black artist who exhibits internationally, has related several experiences of curatorial intervention. B. Ross Smith—whose projects include his ongoing series *Our Kind of People,* a community-sourced and -focused recurring installation; *Got The Power: Boomboxes;* and the powerful collaborative work *Question Bridge: Black Males*—shared several experiences surrounding *Our Kind of People.* As he recounts, a gallery wanted to reconfigure the series and display the works, as they hadn't previously been arranged, with new juxtapositions that were not the direct correlations he had constructed in previous installations of the series. As B. Ross Smith explains, "I let them do it because I was interested to see how it looked—even though I wasn't that into it."[10] More problematically, the new installation created inferences and dialogues that did not previously exist. B. Ross Smith continues:

> It just really didn't get to the heart of what I was attempting to do with the works. Everyone brings a certain response to a certain face and a certain outfit. And—I think—they made it more into an examination of race, which is definitely part of it, but that depends on who you are. There's definitely a different examination of race depending on your race. And so, it also felt like they were taking a very mainstream, white approach to *Our Kind of People*—which was fine—but they didn't contextualize the installation as "We" or "I."[11]

The result? B. Ross Smith's constructed interconnections would become unintentionally fractured visual and experiential narratives, unmoored from intention, yet aligned closely enough to offer the appearance of exploring how B. Ross Smith's aesthetic communications were relationally connected to audience experiences. Within this curatorially and structurally realigned framework, representation, expectation, and experience would have appeared to be binary. When asked if discussions surrounding this alternative contextualization of *Our Kind of People* had occurred, B. Ross Smith remarked, "I had conversations with them, but they didn't send me the text for approval first. I really wish we would've had a conversation about this."[12]

In many ways, curatorial decision making and its corollary implications are often viewed as having the same significance as the de minimus principle in law. The principle holds that some actions are so insignificant that, when weighed, they are not sufficient to impact the matter under consideration. Viewed holistically, a de minimus principle should never extend to the visual arts. If intentionality operates from creation through completion, it must operate holistically. This conceptual framework has not changed.

Instead, perceptions of significance have shifted. Rather than meaning being encompassed within the creative object, today the artwork's impacts and implications are disseminated across every element of an exhibition. As a result, unless an artist asserts categorical ownership over an exhibition's ancillary components, these fall within the curatorial purview. This indeterminacy between where a work begins and ends—its materiality versus its scope and range—creates what one might term "curatorial creep": a slow shift in agency that occurs, little by little, as decisions that might have been integral for some (think Marcel Broodthaers) become less so. At some point, a delineation between the object and any of its ancillary elements—including exhibition—occurs, shifting responsibility for everything but the work itself from artist to curator. What results is the experiential break between the two. "It was completely her choice," "You know that doesn't happen," "You know, I really wish we would've had a conversation about this."

Curatorial intervention can emerge as a lure to entice an artist to return to a prior visual language. In these moments, curators question current practices and gently urge artists to work in specific ways. This is a David-versus-Goliath battle that occurs on the ground between an artist's "signature style" and their need for creative experimentation. In 2015, the New Zealand artist Terry Urbahn recounted having been invited to participate in an exhibition, observing:

> [T]here wasn't any opportunity to reconfigure the work or re-present it. So, all of the sudden it got uninteresting. And they were also wanting to overemphasize one artwork as more of a global theme. So, they wanted to exaggerate how much I used the influence of spellmaking in my work, even in the ritualistic way of making the work—trying to make me out as some sort of shaman. And I said, "No, you're going over the top with this." So, it got to a point where I said, "I can't come up with any new ideas around this theme," and didn't take part in that show.

Two questions emerge from this exchange. The first concerns the amount of conceptual elasticity an artist is willing to attribute to their work. Conceptual elasticity is the extent to which an artist might be willing to allow a curator to recontextualize their work or project so it can be situated within an alternative theoretical or curatorial context. The second considers how willing artists may be to "manufacture" meaning after the fact—in essence, to conceptually reconfigure themselves, to reposition their own agency relative to new dialogues within which curators may be situating their work and, by extension, themselves.

For existing work, the operation of conceptual elasticity may mean interpreting art outside its original intentions. And, while art is not static, it is not endlessly pliable either—its meanings cannot be stretched to fill any thematic within which a curator would like to situate it. At some point, artworks must, metaphorically, succumb to Hooke's Law, first stated in "The True Theory of Elasticity and Springiness" (1676): *ut tension, sic vis*, or "as extension, so force." In Urbahn's case, this elasticity extended to the limit at which the work in question could no longer have returned to its original intentionality. This becomes significant because it suggests that within the action of curatorial intervention we may encounter this variable—elasticity—and have to determine what will emerge not as a determination of occurrence but an evaluation of degree.

Consider, for a moment, an artist whose works have been the subject of seemingly endless conceptual elasticity: Pablo Picasso. In 2015, *Picasso.Mania* at the Grand Palais in Paris, France, explored the influence of Picasso on painting, sculpture, film, and advertising. Much of the show was installed salon style (to reference Picasso's 1970 exhibition at Avignon),[13] and, at the time of this more recent exhibition, curator Didier Ottinger noted that the premise of the show was risky because there was a chance artists would not want their works directly compared with Picasso. As Ottinger noted:

> The purpose was to study the legacy of Picasso, not just through visual art but also through cinema, through music and even advertising, which is something huge because Picasso seems to be everywhere. We wanted to emphasise this very specific dimension of Picasso, which is that he is not only a painter but a man responsible for incarnating the genius of the 20th and now 21st century.[14]

Not surprisingly, Urbahn's experience was anything but isolated. The Australian-based New Zealand artist Ronnie Van Hout, whose major survey exhibition inaugurated Melbourne's Buxton Contemporary in 2018, shared—rather self-deprecatingly—how curators have at times approached his works. Van Hout's unnerving, quasi-autobiographical works positioned him as the *enfant terrible* of mid- to late-1990s New Zealand art. He has relentlessly pursued his own creative interests, even when the results were challenging and—at times—challenging conceptually, curatorially, and economically. Throughout, Van Hout has remained laconic and undeterred. In 2015, Van Hout offered, rather wryly, that at times he can be approached regarding the exhibition of works he's moved beyond. He recounts that he will be asked, "Actually—aren't you making any of those figures anymore?" To which he had once replied, "No one was interested in them. So, I moved on." The response? "Well, it would be great if you could do one of those."[15]

In fact, Van Hout refuses to define his "signature style," a signifier attached to artists from Ernst Kirschner to Janet Cardiff and George Bures Miller: "Cardiff's signature style of combining narrative fragments with stream-of-consciousness remarks evokes both wonder and bewilderment in participants."[16] Instead, Van Hout's works teeter as if a more disheveled subject that had escaped from a Dinos and Jake Chapman installation was strolling down Cuba Street in Wellington, New Zealand. Recently, his hybrid giant hand and self-portrait, the sixteen-foot-tall Quasi, disturbed viewers across the capital city's center. Meme worthy, the work turned up on Hypebeast.com,[17] where it included a screen capture of one viewer's tweet, with the very valid question, "What the fuck is this nightmare?"[18]

Think about these experiences. Urban and Van Hout aren't discussing the commission of new works; they aren't discussing current projects; they aren't even discussing exhibiting existing works in contemporary contexts. Instead, they are being asked to consider a practice-based shift away from current interests and concerns to refabricate or reconstruct pieces, ideas, or processes they no longer explore. These types of requests are unavoidable in part because the very practice of curating is ex post facto—first, the need to archive, catalog, and consider, and then additional need to comment, construct, and contextualize. So the weight of evaluating the existence and implications of a "what was" is balanced by expectations of the "what is," making the process of curating even more asynchronous. At times, these dialogues occur in the space of a studio visit—one of the most contested sites for curatorial intervention.

Perhaps the issue hinges on what the artwork contains. How much meaning does a work have at each stage of its journey from inception to presentation? To situate this fully, we must return to reception aesthetics where, according to Hans Robert Jauss, aesthetic exchange is fixed between object and viewer. This should mean that curators would not be able to mediate work at any point in its journey from inception to reception. Yet clearly this is not the case. For our purposes, to account for this anomaly, the curator is inserted into the aesthetic exchange somewhere along its continuum. The question is, where?

First, contemplate that twentieth-century theories surrounding intention and reception always structured the exchange as binary. Wolfgang Kemp goes so far as to suggest that the relationship between artist and audience is always indeterminate—and it is the role of the audience to complete artists' works. Kemp writes:

> Works of art are unfinished in themselves in order to be finished by the beholder (Ingarden 1965, Iser 1978, Kemp 1985). This state of unfinishedness or indeterminacy is constructed and intentional. But it does mean that as spectators we must complete the invisible reverse side of each represented figure, or that we mentally continue a path that is cut off by the frame. In this way, everyday perception is no different from aesthetic perception. The work of art lays a claim to coherence, though, and this impulse turns its "blanks" into important links or causes for constituting meaning.[19]

This binary exchange is crucial. Kemp had earlier observed:

> In the same way that the beholder approaches the work of art, the work of art approaches him, responding to and recognizing the activity of his perception. What he will find first is a contemplating figure on the other side of the divide. This recognition, in other words, is the most felicitous pointer to the most important premise of reception aesthetics: namely, that the function of beholding has already been incorporated into the work itself.[20]

Clearly, then, Kemp perceives that it is not curators, but viewers, who are "incorporated into the work." For curatorial intervention to occur, curators must be seen as integral rather than supplemental to this theoretically binary exchange. What allows this to occur is the structural nature of the art exchange itself, which adds an additional layer between what had formerly been an immediate exchange. In fact, it is the construction and control of space, rather than solely the function of title, that first allows intervention to occur.

At times, the disparate nature of the binary exchange becomes further problematized through the construct of social or audience obligation. Accessibility situates the majority of community/museum exchanges today, theorized in anthologies like "Museums and Communities," and formalized through institutions such as the San Jose Museum of Art and History, particularly during its "museum as engagement incubator" phase under the directorship of Nina Simon. Sophia Krzys Acord emphasizes the problematics that ensue, particularly when curators are conceptually or programmatically distanced from an institution's accessibility mandate. Acord explains, "Hence, museum curators become responsible for what sociologist Nathalie Heinich terms 'managing the irreconcilable,' negotiating the contradiction between the civic logic of institutions working in the public interest, and the contemporary artistic logic of transgressing established traditions, and challenging audiences to think critically about civic institutions."[21]

This experiential construct—the artist–audience dialogue, seen through the lens of an institutional frame, adds a layer of unexpected complexity to dualistic reception. Richard Schechner, professor emeritus of performance studies at New York University and editor of the influential journal *TDR: The Drama Review*, suggested that reception can exist outside and beyond the immediacy of aesthetic experience. He writes, "[a] performance is a 'was' even as it occurs; its value is mostly as a 'was.' The 'owners of meaning' are those who construct the aftermath where was is."[22] Conceptually, an exhibition's reception exists partially within this "was"—in the space of the supplement, curatorial statements, ephemera, catalogs, and documentary experiences that establish the existence of an event outside a direct encounter with the viewer. While Jauss's theory does not address Schechner's hypothesis of the "experience outside the experience" (what one might term Schechner's aftereffect) either as a going-beyond or as a repeat encounter, he does imply Walter Benjamin's copy without the original from *The Work of Art in the Age of Mechanical Reproduction*: "[f]rom a photographic negative, for example, one can make any number of prints; to ask for the 'authentic' print makes no sense."[23] Reception theory, then displaces the "authentic" for the subjective, while anchoring reception with experience. Schechner's experiential hypothesis could just as easily suggest Friedrich Nietzsche's eternal return and Jean Baudrillard's "hell of the same."[24] Baudrillard speaks of how cloning flattens affect. He remarks, "the Other as gaze, the Other as mirror, the Other as opacity—all are gone. Henceforward it is the transparency of others that represents absolute danger."[25] This triumvirate of the other, gaze, mirror, opacity, is synonymous with an interventionist theory beyond reception, with artist/mirror, audience/gaze, and curator/opacity. The Schechnerian experience beyond the experience, the Nietzschean eternal return, and the Baudrillardian trilogy each construct dynamics in which curatorial intervention could, hypothetically, occur. Each also resonates with a Deleuzian exploration and conception of the construction of dramatization. As Jean-Paul Martinon observes in *The Curatorial*:

> The exhibition, the gallery or museum, the talk, the theatre, the screening and so on, all of these things—provide a structural framework that pre-exists the encounter with the body but they do so as a kind of virtual or possible that is itself dramatised through the encounter with the body. In this way, the sensible stage proposes a path between the emergent intensity of Deleuze's dramatization and Badiou's articulation of theatre as the meeting of bodies and text.[26]

The physical and conceptual bodies may each serve as contested sites upon which curatorial intervention occurs. Each is a space for dynamic artist–curator exchanges removed from the audience's observation—although generative of their later perceptions. The body becomes representation, manifestation, and contestation. The Australian artist Brad Buckley, whose ongoing series *The Slaughterhouse Project* interrogates cultural, political, social, and sexual mores—including the objectified body, the body politic, and representations of the body—recounted an instance in which the very inference of the absent body was of grave concern.

Buckley, who also often deconstructs national identities, explains. Having been invited to exhibit in Japan, "the curator asked that I not use the Japanese flag as it would create problems with nationalists." When asked if he complied, he explained that their collaborative dialogue had begun by his sharing the genesis of the first work he had considered installing: "We started with a discussion about a work which explored how the Japanese had killed my uncle—who I am named after—in Burma, when he was a prisoner of war. This seemed to worry him." Undeterred, their discourse continued: "We then moved to the idea of the extended flag piece, which he thought was provocative—but would work well in the university gallery. Later, he asked if I intended to use the Japanese flag. Without saying so, he obviously had reservations." As it transpired, the curator's concerns were well founded. "He told me of a recent incident in which activists had killed a professor who was translating Salman Rushdie's *The Satanic Verses*. When I asked about the situation, he replied, 'It was very inconvenient for the university.'" On July 12, 1991, Japanese academic and translator Hitoshi Igarishi had in fact been found dead in a hallway outside his office at Tsukuba University. When asked if discussions surrounding which flag would be included in the project were in any way made public, Buckley responded, "No, and the flag work—and, also the video—created quite a stir anyway."[27]

Of course, questions emerge concerning potential for curators to intervene in artists' works. Some artists—particularly those who are more established—have suggested that curators' intentions and interventions can, largely, be irrelevant. Remember, Buren asserts he can work against the stupidity of a curator.[28] Here, Buren situates the lack, the fault—the stupidity—to the curator rather than the audience. All too often, this is not the case. Theater, essentially, depends upon an agreement with the audience—hence, aesthetic distance. Magic, hypnosis, and sleights of hand depend upon our easily manipulated powers of perception. But, generally, the art experience is not aesthetically distanced, nor does it prey upon our limited powers of observation. When Buren utters the signifier's "stupidity," he suggests otherwise: "I can do my work even if the curator shows he did not catch a thing." Imagine this doubling—curatorial intervention driven by misperception or misinterpretation—and consider, momentarily, those implications for both work and audience experience.

This is not altogether that far-fetched given the minute gap between meaning and perception. In 1992, in an essay to revisit his statement for *documenta 5,* Daniel Buren commented:

> It's almost grotesque to see how exhibitions are increasingly becoming opportunities for an organizer or a curator or whoever to write an essay which usually has nothing to do with the artists invited, but concerns only his or her philosophy about art and society, politics or aesthetics. Exhibitions focus increasingly univocally on who makes the show, and we can see that the artists chosen to "illustrate" his/her theory are mainly the same from one exhibition to the next. So the very same works are, show after show, illustrating extremely different themes or theories, without any problem. In fact, and this is quite reassuring, no one cares—starting with the artists themselves—about the discourse produced by these exhibition organizers. The only ones who pay attention to and speak about the organizers are the organizers themselves, or art critics who don't speak about the artists in the exhibition so much as about the organizer, perhaps dreaming secretly to be an organizer of exhibitions themselves.[29]

Opportunities—to write something disconnected with the artists, centered upon individuated philosophies of art and society, and revolving around a limited group of practitioners whose creative output are utilized to support any number of divergent themes. Most disturbingly: "no one cares—starting with the artists themselves." Arguable, and Buren can be known for his didactic positioning and incendiary rhetoric, but he reanimates the core disparity between intentionality and interventionality, leading to a reception for which there never was truly an audience apart from, in Buren's opinion, a select group of like-minded curators waiting their turns to share constructions of various hyper-focused curatorial frames.

As Van Hout once remarked, rather ironically, "I remember there were many times you'd go, 'I think this work is about this,'—you'd be talking about your own work—and they'd go, 'No, no. That's not it. That's not what it's about.'" In an interview subsequent to his 2018 mini-retrospective at Buxton Contemporary in Melbourne, Australia, Van Hout and Megan Dunn shared the following exchange:

> Megan Dunn: What did curator Melissa Keys add or subtract from *No One Is Watching You?* Did you have to kill any darlings?
>
> Ronnie van Hout: I once had my fortune told, and I came away with the impression that the theme of my life was "You can't always get what you want, but you just might find you get what you need" which at the time seemed a bit disappointing, but putting together the exhibition I've come to understand it in a different way. In terms of selecting the works, it was often a case of not necessarily getting what you want, realising, and being reminded constantly, that nothing will ever be perfect, so let's learn to love what we have, and what we could afford to loan, make, or dig out in the short time frame we had available to us.[30]

And yet, I would argue, what is at stake is far more a question of value than of occurrence. By now, the notion of curatorial intervention should be coming into focus. And while its particularities and peculiarities remain to be more fully defined, it seems clear that what will be as much at stake, if not more, is the degree to which artists are willing to allow their work to be mediated. As Bayeté Ross Smith so astutely observed:

> What you're talking about is subtle shifts. It's not necessarily the overall project. It's an aspect of it—and you have to decide whether that aspect is worth fighting for or whether we should just get the general benefits of participating in whichever event that it is. (B. Ross Smith, interview with the author, 2016.)

In her 2010 dissertation research, art historian Lucy Cotter outlined a theory of narrative intervention in relation to the construction of exhibitions.[31] This concept, in part, does address an element of curatorial intervention. If curatorial intervention stands as the overarching construct, then various micro-interventions—alterations to the artist's narrative, a redefinition of the exhibition space either physically or conceptually, or a change in the realization of the work from artist's concept to institutional manifestation—each define one potential element where intervention may operate. One of the key challenges within curatorial intervention is recognizing that, while its operation is all-or-nothing, its visibility is not. Any intervention along a continuity from concept to outcome is evident of intervention's operation and impact. But, one need not intervene everywhere for the dynamic to have occurred.

NOTES

1. von Bismarck, "'The Master of the Works': Daniel Buren's Contribution to *documenta 5* in Kassel, 1972," 57.
2. Zerocv, "An Interview with Daniel Buren," 178–79.
3. Smith, interview with the author, February 28, 2016.
4. Ibid.
5. O'Doherty, *Inside the White Cube: The Ideology of the Gallery Space*, 25. O'Doherty's more comprehensive observation is, "When William C. Seitz took off the frames for his great Monet show at the Museum of Modern Art in 1960, the undressed canvasses looked a bit like reproductions until you saw how they began to hold the wall. Though the hanging had its eccentric moments, it read the pictures' relation to the wall correctly and, in a rare act of curatorial daring, followed up the implications. Seitz also set some of the Monets flush with the wall. Continuous with the wall, the pictures took on some of the rigidity of tiny murals. The surfaces turned hard as the picture plane was 'overliteralized.' The difference between the easel picture and the mural was clarified."
6. Hendeles, "Curatorial Compositions," 362–63.
7. Zangwill, "Art and Audience," 315.
8. O'Neill, "The Co-Dependent Curator."
9. Michel Foucault (1966, 1970). *The Order of Things*. Routledge: London.
10. Ross Smith, interview with the author, 2016.
11. Ibid.
12. Ibid.
13. Solway, "Picasso Mania."
14. Didier Ottinger, quoted in Hannah Ellis-Peterson, "Paris Exhibition Explores Wide-reaching Influence of Pablo Picasso," *The Guardian*, October 7, 2015. https://www.theguardian.com/artanddesign/2015/oct/07/paris-exhibition-influence-of-pablo-picasso-mania
15. Ronnie Van Hout, interview with the author, August 27, 2015.
16. Copeland, "Aural Sensation: Janet Cardiff and George Bures Miller," 30.
17. Keith Estiler, 2019. "Artist's Giant Hand Sculpture Causes Nightmares in New Zealand." Hypebeast. https://hypebeast.com/2019/8/ronnie-van-hout-quasi-hand-sculpture-city-gallery-wellington-new-zealand
18. Ibid.
19. Kemp, "The Work of Art and Its Beholder: The Methodology and Aesthetic of Reception," 188.
20. Ibid., 181.
21. Acord, "Guest Curating in the Museum: Lost in Translation?"
22. Schechner, "Ways of Speaking, Loci of Cognition," 6.
23. Benjamin, "The Work of Art in the Age of Mechanical Reproduction," 224.
24. Baudrillard, *The Transparency of Evil: Essays on Extreme Phenomena*, 113.
25. Ibid., 122.
26. Jean-Paul Martinon (2013). *The Curatorial*. Kindle loc. 3859–63.
27. Weisman, "Japanese Translator of Rushdie Book Found Slain."
28. Zerocv, "An Interview with Daniel Buren," 178–79.
29. Fox, "Being Curated."
30. Dunn and van Hout, "Bad Dads: An Interview with Ronnie van Hout and Megan Dunn," 42.
31. Cotter, *Curating, Cultural Capital and Symbolic Power: Representations of Irish Art in London, 1950–2010.*

THREE

Errata Minimalia

In 2000, speaking at the *Curating Now: Imaginative Practice/Public Responsibility* symposium, the curator and educator Robert Storr made a remarkable admission:

> I have abiding doubts about many aspects of the relation of modern and contemporary art to the museums and other venues devoted to them. Those doubts become specific when I consider the ways in which what I, in all good will, do as a curator may qualify or denature what the artist has tried to do. This is not a simple problem, and walking away from it won't help matters. All things considered, I would rather be in a position where I can test certain options, in the service of what I believe in and what I think the artist believes in, and use my intuition and expertise to try to minimize the mistakes that can be made in presenting their work than to stand back and let someone else run those risks and indulge myself in the luxury of being right about how they were wrong. The fact is, I have been responsible for having "framed" or contextualized art in ways that subtly, albeit unintentionally, altered its meaning or diminished its impact. As a practicing curator, one has to be straightforward not only about the potential for but the likelihood of doing this in a given circumstance.[1]

What precisely did Storr mean? "Those doubts become specific when I consider the ways in which what I, in all good will, do as a curator may qualify or denature what the artist has tried to do." He continues, outlining how he prefers, generally, to "test certain options, in the service of what I believe in," trying, as it were, to "minimize the mistakes that can be made in presenting their work." He reveals that his practices may have "subtly, albeit unintentionally," contextualized or framed works in ways which altered their meanings or diminished their impacts.

These alterations, these impacts, could occur because of a willingness to potentially situate works within a curatorial construct that required their elasticity—with the impact mitigated attempting to "minimize the mistakes." A close reading shows that his interventions emerge, in Storr's words, "in the service of what I believe in and what I think the artist believes." Storr acts on an inference, to the extent that his belief is not necessarily based on what the artist believes, but on an inference drawn from what he *thinks* they believe—he presents what he believes which should align not with belief, but with intent. And, despite these assertions, the artist's intentions remain elusive. Storr's curatorial construct cannot derive precisely from the artist's intentions, but builds from his own interpretations. This concept of curatorial reinterpretation situates artists' works on the periphery, where they become illustrative tools for constructed narratives. Storr's beliefs and perceptions regarding exhibitions for which he feels this way emerge as preeminent—although they are founded on inference as much as on understanding. And, while Storr may be one of a small number of iconoclastic, innovative curators testing the limits of intention, intervention, and reception, his perceived conflation of the primacy of curatorial perceptions contra to, or in supplement of, artists' intentions, seems predominantly to prevail.

Storr's interpositioning of a curator between the dialectic of artist and viewer suggests a divergent approach to considering reception. As Peter Sloterdijk observes, "The modality, or genre, presents just as important a role for understanding the writing as deciphering the original text."[2] Storr's modality becomes a counternarrative as important as the artist's intent—perhaps more so.

Storr's narrative establishes first a subjective and individuated space. Philosophically, this space mirrors the overarching realm of subjectivity and reinforces the fundamentally individuated experience of reception. While the construct can be communal, in fact the outcome is, by necessity, a singular response to a sole object. Curating occupies a space between the two. Perhaps curator and writer Matthew Higgs, director of White Columns in New York, identified this gap simply as interstitial, as a space. In *The Edge of Everything: Reflections on Curatorial Practice*, he remarks, "Between the audience and the stage, between the spectacle and its reception, there exists a 'space,' a tangible if undefinable space in which to operate. It is this space that interests me, and it is this space that I continue to negotiate."[3]

This counternarrative need not necessarily be opaque. Robert Leonard, now chief curator at City Gallery, Wellington, has held positions including directorships at New Zealand's Artspace, in Auckland, and Australia's Institute of Modern Art, in Brisbane. Twice, he has curated the New Zealand commission for the Venice Biennale and, in the early 1990s, co-curated the groundbreaking *Headlands: Thinking Through New Zealand Art*. Leonard regards explored curatorial intervention as creating opportunities to explore creative and curatorial potential. As he explains:

> I started curating . . . working with collections. There, my approach was informed by "the death of the author." I operated with the view that, so long as you didn't hang a work upside down, you could present it in perverse company and make it operate in ways that were outside the scope of the artist's intention. Back then, I thought the role of the curator was to take such liberties.[4] (Robert Leonard, interview with the author, August 12, 2015)

In subsequent exchanges, Leonard discussed these ideas further, outlining how the role of a contemporary curator hinges upon both autonomy and agency. Leonard differentiates between working with collections and artists, outlining how his perceptions shift when working autonomously versus collaboratively. He also discussed how one might work collaboratively with both collections and artists.

Leonard remarked that, over the course of his career, his scope to explore complex issues has become more constrained. This constraint illustrates how dramatically interventionist frameworks—or perhaps, more elastically, interpretationalist frameworks—ground critically informed dialogues between artist, work, frame, and audience. As Leonard explains, "A lot of what you are describing comes down to ethics—the ethical relation between curators and artists, and institutions and publics. I want to take opportunities to advance my own enquiry. I think that's the pathway to making better exhibitions."[5]

Of course, having opportunities to explore individual curatorial inquiries emerges from experience. This is how Leonard best situates an engaging practice that can offer opportunities to pursue one's critically driven ideas. This is curating from a position of risk—a model one could assert that Leonard embodies. Not unmitigated, uninformed risk, but a willingness to follow a thread of interpretation that was previously hidden. Bishop has explored similar questions, as she does in her 2007 essay, "What Is a Curator?" where she dissects the famous letter signed by 10 artists protesting curator Harald Szeemann's curatorial vision for *documenta 5*. She then supplements this with an examination of Robert Smithson's essay "Cultural Confinement," published in the same catalog, and Robert Morris's missive withdrawing from the show. In each instance, the impetus for their actions was their perception of an overreach by the curator, Harald Szeemann. In more contemporary contexts, we would perceive these approaches as being precisely those sorts of risk-taking examinations that Leonard at least posits as significant positions for a curator to take. Bishop resolves these remarks on *documenta 5* thus:

> What Morris wants from a curator is someone who respects the artist's wishes, communicates clearly, and is available for negotiation. In other words, a figure who is subservient to the artist and who does not contest his/her authorship. There is no clearer way to grasp these expectations than to imagine these complaints applied to an installation, or to an artist-curated exhibition. Although both curating and installation

> are concerned with selection, they function within different discursive spheres: curatorial selection is always an ethical negotiation of pre-existing authorships, rather than the artistic creation of meaning sui generis.[6]

There's that word again—ethics. That responsibility that lies within the negotiation between artist and curator. What lies before, however, is even more complex, for before one can negotiate ethics, one must negotiate its operation. What is at stake here is the very nature of intervention before one discusses its values. In a sense, it becomes Nietzschean, it becomes the revaluation of curatorial values when, in fact, it is their renegotiation. Consider, for a moment, the ethics of agreement. Here is Ivan Gaskell, speaking at the symposium *How Museums Do Things with Artworks*:

> When discussing display we may disagree among ourselves about the specific use of any given artwork on a particular occasion, even to the extent of believing that its maker's intentions are being betrayed, but the multivalency of artworks, and the temporary nature of any such display, should allay any fears that irreparable harm is being done.[7]

And here is Joseph Del Pesco, program director of the Kadist Foundation in San Francisco, who describes the extant framework of the exhibition as an "exhausted format," asserting that audiences are either oblivious to, or overinfluenced by, the narratives that curators devise.[8] Del Pesco proposes, but does not define, something he describes—archly—as "not-exhibitions," although what they would be, how curators would be positioned within them, or how they would engage with audiences is unclear. Furthermore, the nomenclature of "not-exhibition" would not necessarily displace the curator from a position of authorship. It would merely reposition them within a contextual space and assign an/other name.

This space could very easily emerge as a nuanced space in which the specificities of curatorial ethics, and by extension curatorial intervention, are subjective. In a dialogue with Aaron Seeto, former curator of the Queensland Art Gallery/Gallery of Modern Art, now director of Museum MACAN in Jakarta, Indonesia:

> When I read the questions you sent, I was thinking their framing implies a very particular kind of curatorship. When I have taught curatorial studies students in the past, I have always identified the many different types of curators. You could be working for a private collector with narrow interests, or, you could be a curator working for an auction house, a public institution, or an independent space. All of these situations have different historical contexts, and they demand what I would call different ethical approaches. It's not necessarily a question of whether one is being more or less interventionist; it's a question of, "What are the ethical boundaries?" Those ethical boundaries, I think, are determined by the broader cultural, political, and social contexts which surround those individual spaces.[9]

Repeatedly, the issue emerges in this manner—not as a universal issue mandating how curators should situate themselves in relation to questions of curatorial intervention. Instead, Leonard, Bishop, and Seeto each outline a theoretical framework of limits against which intervention might be measured. This extends far beyond mere questions of occurrence. Here, these frameworks structure dialogues that situate dialogues operating with several concurrent variables, including, but not limited to, curatorial agency, intentionality, and motivation; curatorial ethics; artistic agency and power; and conceptual and creative elasticity, both curatorial and creative. In fact, what Seeto does very eloquently is shift a problematic dialogue to a positive one. His critique that the problematics of curatorial intervention is not without merit. But, one must situate the problem before one may extend it. With that, his capacity to then distill intervention into even more critical elements was exceptional. As he notes, there must be differentiations between those interventions that operate against an artist's intention, and those that seek to further their objectives—a goal that underpins most, if not all, of its operations. Seeto had served as the director of the Asian Australian Artists Alliance, known as 4A, in Sydney, Australia. Commenting on his approach retrospectively, he remarked:

> As a director . . . sometimes I found that the situation required different kinds of input. I wasn't the artist, but my role as a curator was to really try and push the meanings of works in different ways. Or, to play the role as a commissioner, because that was the other thing that we would do—find pots of money for artists to make things. It was an opportunity for us to really look at what an artist may have been dreaming about, but not necessarily had the opportunity to fully conceptualise, or never had the money to actually produce. So, the role I think then of the director, the commissioner, and the curator is quite interesting, and it necessitates a type of intervention.[10]

What if one were to map these shifts? They would move from intention and reception through intervention as allusion, to intervention as possibility, to intervention as positive operation. And yet, these shifts occur without any external referent. The problematics that arise are not just revealed in curatorial intervention's operation, but also through its (in)visibility. This is a significant distinction to draw in part because the roles curators play in facilitating the realization of works can be of immeasurable value. Think, for example, of organizations such as the Public Art Fund in New York or Sydney's John Kaldor Public Art Projects. These organizations are renowned funding organizations with renowned curators working tirelessly to facilitate major projects: in New York, first Nicholas Baume, then Suzy Delvalle, served artists' interests. If one applies Seeto's model above, what results is a positive model of intervention, one that is grounded in the role of fostering opportunities.

Still, curatorial intervention and its operations are as elusive as they are elastic. For curatorial intervention to be comprehensively interrogated, both the function and framework of the curator must be considered. Curatorial intervention is one extension of this function. Function—the defining set of rules and practices that situate curating—contextualizes intervention, shifting any analysis of intervention from a simple yes or no judgment to interrogations of "how, when, and why." If a pronouncement on curatorial intervention were as simple as evaluating action, capable of being answered in the negative or the affirmative to questions such as "Have you done this?" then the operation of curatorial intervention would be of limited significance. Instead, time and again artists experience the curator, and by extension the museum/institution, as an active participant in previously diametric and dialectic relationships between artist and audience.

As significantly, curatorial intervention is not defined by a single mode of operation. Instead, it can emerge across multiple aspects of curatorial practice, each with unique implications. First, at times there can be the impression that curatorial constructs can operate in parallel with intentionality. This potential emerges in statements by curators such as Gaskell, above, who spoke of betrayed intentions, "multivalency," and allaying "fears that irreparable harm is being done."[11] In a multivalent approach, both artist and artwork become objectified. Each may be contextualized within changing intellectual frameworks and inserted variously into contexts constructed by curators. Both artist and object are at the service of the curator's intellectual, critical, social, cultural, and philosophical constructions, albeit with the caveat that no "irreparable harm" be done.[12] This notion of "irreparable harm" suggests that Gaskell perceives the viewing experience to be detached from the art object. Otherwise, audiences would attach specific meanings to the works they see, and contextualizing a work outside its intended meaning would likely cause irreparable harm. In Gaskell's model, audience experience exists somewhere between flash blindness and residual memory: the impact of the misrepresented work will fade, its decontextualization of little lasting impact, leaving only the ever-fading aftereffect that situated the object's reception somewhere unintended. One might argue that this is wholly interventionist.

An alternative—though still interventionist—approach proposes that curators mediate both the object and the experience as little as possible. To appreciate this distinction, you have to situate curatorial intervention against exhibition practice. Then, you overlay intervention and determine the requisite level of transparency. This offers two potential outcomes. In an interview with Gerd Elise Mørland and Heide Bale Amundsen, Simon Sheikh considers this interventionist framework, remarking:

> You mentioned the difference between alternative spaces of self-organization and large-scale exhibitions like the biennial. In a way these are two ends of the economic ladder. The problem is that it's almost impossible to compare them. These two exhibition forms are somehow loosely connected in what we call "the artworld," and certain agents in the artworld are going for both of them. This goes for both artists and curators, you could be in a biennial one day, and in an alternative space the next. Not just at different stages in your career, but also within the same year, or even at the same moment. And both formats might fit well into each other. But again, the problem is in terms of the reception, that they're presented to the public as if the exhibitions were made as fully formed articulations, and obviously they are not, they are both based on a lot of constrains [sic]. And specifically when it comes to alternative or self-organized exhibitions. Here, I am also drawing from my own experience of having worked within this context. The exhibition is perceived in the media, and sometimes by the audience as well, as belonging to the same public and as being produced in the same way as a museum exhibition. And therefore it is considered under produced. But you obviously can't compare these formats because they don't have the brief or the same economy.[13]

Think of Sheikh's construct as mediated intervention. In Gaskell's model, curatorial intervention can be either marginal or significant. Its elasticity revolves around the level of reinterpretation through representation of an extant object within a specific exhibition context. For Sheikh, the problem that curatorial intervention presents is that audiences often encounter works with the belief that everything that goes into their construction is essentially the same. Or you could *artwash* it—strip the work of its creative contextualization—a practice not entirely unimaginable in neoliberal institutions. An extension to Sheikh's model would be one in which the exhibition participants—the familiar conceptual linearity of artist–curator–audience—is deemed passé.

Third, there is the potential to leverage a collaborative site as interventionist practice given its role in defining the artist–audience relationship. As Namita Gupta Wiggers, former director of the Museum of Contemporary Craft and now the director of the MA program in historical craft studies at Warren Wilson College, explains, "I basically approach every encounter and environment as an opportunity to rethink curatorial practice. My iPhone, laptop and iPad are the most productive tools to access people, images and discourse and to prompt conversations that lead to curatorial projects."[14]

Finally, curatorial intervention can be driven externally. While the *documenta 5* artists issued their demands and made their assessments of Szeemann's practice relative to its impacts on their individual works, at times a collective artistic approach drives curators to address specific social or cultural issues. In their 2015 essay "Request for a Radical Redefinition: Curatorial Politics after Institutional Critique," Amundsen and

Morland summarize the many competing demands Juliana Engberg had to consider as she assessed her curatorial frame for the 2014 *Biennale of Sydney*. There, problems regarding the exhibition's longtime and major funder emerged—not as a result of their commitment to Australian art, but instead, from a subsidiary's actions relative to the larger social issue of refugee detention.[15] That patron, Transfield Holdings, owned a subsidiary that operated an immigration detention facility in Nauru and had recently been awarded the contract to operate another on Manus Island. Twenty-eight artists wrote a letter in protest, and a total of 10 participating artists withdrew as a result.[16] There, a question just as puzzling emerges—is this a shift from the "Morris-style" letter asserting individuated professional concerns to the expression of a collective artistic intentionality that could destabilize, or even displace, curatorial conceptualization? And what would the implications for curatorial intervention be? Would the intentionality emerging in the artists' letter from *documenta 5* finally spring to life?

In fact, this collective creative consciousness occurring contemporaneous with individual intentionality is more and more frequent: in Engberg's 2014 *Biennale of Sydney*, the 2019 *Whitney Biennial*, and the recently canceled Whitney exhibition on Black culture and collective identity, to cite merely three examples. Throughout the *Biennale of Sydney* challenges, Engberg struggled against the capital–creative complex that obscured the politics surrounding Australia's treatment of refugees. She found herself squeezed between the *Biennale of Sydney*'s largest (and longest) patron and major funder, Transfield Holdings; its subsidiary, Transfield Services; and the *Biennale*'s longest and most generous patron, the Belgiorno Nettis family. In the end, collective consciousness triumphed over a perceived cultural callousness—although the implications of alienating a cultural organization's most significant sponsor seem challenging to overcome long term. For the 2019 *Whitney Biennial*, the question of representation underpinned a revaluation of Black value—not Black values, but a concrete dialogue regarding how best to negotiate representations of diversity and inclusion for Black, indigenous, and people of color voices, as well as those of other underrepresented populations within the museum would be represented, as well as the collaborations that would drive these dialogues.

What each of the four positions above represents is one possible construction of curatorial intervention—and how each compels the curator to occupy a unique space. In the first, which could be termed a multivalent approach, both the artist and the artwork (or artefact) can be termed objects situated within larger frameworks or intellectual contexts constructed by curators. This would be a completely mediated site, and one that could be considered as wholly interventionist. Here, both the artist and the object are at the total service of the curator for their intellectual, critical, social, cultural, and philosophical constructions, with the caveat, as Gaskell puts it, that no "irreparable harm" is being done.[17] This notion of "irreparable harm" reflects Gaskell's perception that the capacity to fully deconstruct and define the parameters of either exhibition practice or the implications of curatorial intervention would be so challenging that to attempt to do so would be impossible.

And one more consideration: dialogues surrounding curatorial intervention are not primarily motivated by a desire to lift the corporate veil or examine which group of private or foundation donors may have funded the realization of signature works. While curatorial intervention obviously contains aspects of this discourse, except in certain circumstances, the operation of curatorial intervention is not donor–curator–artist. When it is, however, the exchange can be humorous. The Australian installation artist Brad Buckley, well known for his ongoing international series *The Slaughterhouse Project*, once recounted an experience in Lodz, Poland, during which the exhibition's organizers were invited to make a donation to the site where he intended to install his work. At the time, in Buckley's words, he had remarked, "I think he is asking for a bribe." The notion that the literal—as well as political—economies of art could converge in such a moment had implications for the operation of curatorial intervention. And, while Robin Bell may project "Pay Trump Bribes Here" on the façade of the Trump International Hotel in Washington, DC, in actuality artists do not generally anticipate a financial exchange for the opportunity to exhibit during an international exhibition.

Still, at times Buckley's works had been the subject of other, more direct interventions—and not at the hands of curators:

> 1995 was the Year of Peace—which is rather ironic now looking back after twenty years. The fact was that there was great optimism then because the borders with Jordan were actually open. In terms of installing the work, when we got there, it was people who were committed to the whole idea of Construction in Process Israel. They facilitated the special flagpoles and us putting the flags up. They made the Israeli flag in the colors of the P.L.O., and vice-versa. You can imagine it was controversial in Israel. The flagpoles were manufactured so they weren't normal flagpoles where you could raise and lower flags. They had U-shaped steel eyelets at the top of each pole. So, we put the flags up using a cherry-picker and I tied them up. The idea was once we put them up they would stay up. And because you couldn't get at them, they were up for a few days. And then we came back, and someone had actually cut the flagpoles down at the base with an angle grinder. So, what was left was the concrete foundation with these two round holes in it, which I rather liked actually.[18]

But to return to the issue at hand. The questions revolve around two primary loci: one, how interventionist should curators be? Two, how transparent should those interventions be to audiences? A third thread to tease must be how curators—and administrators, particularly museum directors—position themselves relative to the dynamic framework of artist–curator. In Leonard's model, one might argue that the theoretical narrative is curatorially situated—the ideation emerges from an observation, an interrogation, or a dialogue that Leonard wishes to generate with, by, and through visual culture. One would imagine that he would agree with Adam Lerner, former director and chief animator (his chosen title) of the Museum of Contemporary Art Denver. Having been asked to define the term *curator*, Lerner remarked:

> I honestly don't care that much, I'm sorry. I know that is the subject matter of your research. I think that what's more important than the definition is what the person is doing—and is that interesting to me? So therefore, technically my title should be director and chief curator but I gave myself the title director and chief animator. And I gave myself that title because in many ways I feel that an animator reflects more of what interests me about my job, because an animator is somebody who brings images to life for people.[19]

Finding a language that can situate this type of practice is problematic—in part because of the antagonisms between the possible and the actual, between how a curator could work, and how, in the examples that are outlined here, curators have worked. And, in some circumstances, there is really no difference between the two. The question is not one of how the work is resolved for the artist: it is one of how it is conveyed to the audience. This distinction is seldom drawn in part because this is where discussions most often diverge. The diversions from traditional, reception-focused theories of curatorial transaction (or lack thereof) are revelatory in part for the lengths to which curators and administrators go to facilitate positive experiences for artists, despite the reality that their interventions are unspoken and opaque: audiences do not see their actions, but their outcomes are manifest. Examining the curatorial practice of Miranda Lash, formerly of the Speed Museum of Art, and now senior curator at the Museum of Contemporary Art Denver, Ivan Gaskell remarked:

> Where Lash uses terms that reinforce the interpersonal collaborations that make each curated project unique—midwife, facilitator, and project manager—other contemporary curators have offered terminology that can feel more romanticized and, in many ways, serve to deflect from the significance of their interventions.[20]

Harald Szeemann referred to his curatorial process as an "adventure";[21] Hou Hanru termed it a "collaboration."[22] Still, Vasif Kortun literally (and figuratively) specifies curatorial practice as intervention.[23] In 2001, Kortun was one of a group of curators beginning to address the power disparities extant in curatorial practice. If we were to return to our common Oxford English Dictionary (OED) definition of I, its very manifestation within curatorial practice would equate to alterity. Per the OED, to intervene is "To come between in action; to interfere, interpose; also, to act as intermediary; to take a share in."[24] And this "coming between in action" is at least twofold, although Liam Gillick offers three: the art market, the curatorial (defined by Gillick as a curator's complete focus), and art as a paradigm of potential.[25] The triangulated construct—crucial for curatorial intervention—also resonates with curator Ingrid Schaffner, although her triumvirate is artist, artwork (not curator), and audience.[26] The problem with Schaffner's structure is its lack of a curator—an omission that fundamentally diverges from Gillick, whose curatorialism, for want of a better term, extends across the range of practices: a market focus, individual expertise (the return of connoisseurship, even), and the opportunity for constructing expression. This construct could be applied universally, detached from the object in favor of an object. A curator would have to situate work within its economic and market frames, construct its connective meanings, and create its extended meanings. Such a frame would be intervention *res extensa*.

As problematically as the notion of expansive interventionism may be, any theory of curatorial intervention must also fundamentally differ from "demystification," which Paul O'Neill describes as having emerged from the mid-1960s writings of Seth Siegelaub. Demystification gained prominence over the subsequent two decades, only to become subsumed by other practices in the 1990s, before being "remystified" in the present day.[27] As O'Neill notes:

> For Siegelaub, demystification was a necessary process in revealing and evaluating the more hidden curatorial components of an exhibition, making evident that the actions of curators had an impact on which artworks were exhibited and how they were produced, mediated, and distributed. In his words, to understand what the curator does is to understand, in part, what you are looking at in an exhibition. As Siegelaub later stated about his generation, "we thought that we could demystify the role of the museum, role of the collector, and the production of artwork; for example, how the size of the gallery affects the production of art, etc."[28]

Demystification could be considered a corollary to curatorial intervention, but not a substitute. Its aims and objections were, and remain, expository rather than actionable. Demystification is not about negotiating curatorial intervention Seemingly, Siegelaub's demystification encompasses every aspect of curatorial practice, becoming an overarching approach that cannot differentiate between the structural implications of visibility and transparency and the individual and individuated implications of curatorial practice. Demystification has the unintended potential to equalize the factual, functional, and philosophical: with information on size and scale; with questions concerning access, choice, and selection;

and with specific, experience-altering decisions made by curators that impact upon the visual experience. Informationally, they may all seem equal, but conceptually and philosophically this cannot be the case. As O'Neill notes, these issues can be more significant within group exhibitions. In his "Co-Productive Exhibition-Making and Three Principal Categories of Organization: The Background, the Middle-Ground and the Foreground," O'Neill writes:

> Since the 1960s, the group exhibition has opened up a range of curatorial approaches to demystify the role of mediation, and as such, has also enabled divergent artistic practices to be exhibited together under a single rubric. The term "demystification" became a recurring trope within art, and curatorial discourse for how the changing conditions of exhibition production were made manifest in the final exhibition-form. Curators, artists and critics were acknowledging the influential mediating component within an exhibition's formation, production and dissemination. Demystification was a necessary process in revealing and evaluating the more hidden curatorial components of an exhibition, making evident that the actions of curators had an impact on which artworks were exhibited and how they were produced, mediated and distributed for the viewer.[29]

What is perhaps most important to distinguish is simply that, operationally, demystification works externally, toward the audience, while intervention is directed internally, toward the artist. The implications of intervention operate on the audience, but the agency and power must first work on the artist, work, or exhibition—the function of power must be executed before its mystifying implications can be revealed.

A more contemporary construct than demystification—and perhaps curatorial intervention by another name—may be the concept of curatorial translation, described in 2016 as a practice that encompassed "principles of categorization, montage, displacement and assembly."[30]

NOTES

1. Storr, "How We Do What We Do. And How We Don't," 5.
2. Harrison, "A Messenger of the Rope: In Conversation with Peter Sloterdijk."
3. Higgs, "Between the Audience and the Stage," 17.
4. Robert Leonard, correspondence with the author, 2015.
5. Ibid.
6. Bishop, "What Is a Curator?," 26.
7. Gaskell, "Being True to Artists," 59.
8. Marincola et al., *Pigeons on the Grass Alas*, 48.
9. Aaron Seeto, interview with the author, March 17, 2016.
10. Ibid.
11. Gaskell, "Being True to Artists," 59.
12. Ibid.
13. Sheikh, "The Potential of Curatorial Articulation," 6.
14. Ibid., 22.

15. Amundsen and Morland, "Request for a Radical Redefinition: Curatorial Politics after Institutional Critique," 26.
16. SBS News, "Biennale of Sydney Cuts Ties with Sponsor Transfield."
17. Gaskell, "Being True to Artists," 59.
18. Brad Buckley, interview with the author, August 2, 2015.
19. Adam Lerner, interview with the author, 2015.
20. Gaskell, "Being True to Artists," 59.
21. Thea, *Foci: Interviews with Ten International Curators*, 19.
22. Ibid., 29.
23. Ibid., 64.
24. Oxford English Dictionary, 1989.
25. Gillick, "The Complete Curator," 26.
26. Marincola et al., *Pigeons on the Grass Alas*, 38.
27. O'Neill, *The Culture of Curating and the Curating of Culture(s)*, 19.
28. Ibid.
29. O'Neill, "Co-Productive Exhibition-Making and Three Principal Categories of Organisation: The Background, the Middle-Ground and the Foreground," 34.
30. Stainforth and Thompson, "Curatorial 'Translations': The Case of Marcel Duchamp's Green Box."

FOUR

Reconfiguring Intervention

There are few places curatorial intervention emerges more evidently than in a museum rehang. This practice, chronicled variously as institutions seeking to address systemic gender, race, and sexual orientation biases, as well as to offer a more "complete" and interrelated history of contemporary art, has become the new proving ground for post-postmodern thinking. Across a range of institutions, including MoMA, and soon, LACMA, reinstallations are exploring new connections and seeking to reveal complex yet previously hidden meanings and interpretations. At times, the process does not seem to go as seamlessly as planned. Take, for example, headlines surrounding the reinstalled Museum of Modern Art, including, "So, is MoMA Woke Now? Not Quite";[1] "The Exuberance of MoMA's Expansion";[2] and Maura Reilly's "MoMA's Revisionism is Piecemeal and Problem-Filled."[3] From the outset, key concerns surrounding MoMA's rehang and reopening focused on opportune versus overlooked narratives—categorized at Artnet.com as a moment when "the curatorial staff has accompanied the expansion with a rehabilitation project, of sorts—a noble attempt to correct lacunae in the collection displays that failed to reflect the truly diverse (i.e., not just white-and-male-and-Eurocentric) nature of the past century and a half of art and how each might emerge." At times, the new narrative seems forced: Faith Ringgold's powerful *American People Series #20: Die, 67*, depicting a bloody street riot, is adjacent (though separated physically by a corner) with Pablo Picasso's *Les Demoiselles d'Avignon*. Museum director Glenn Lowry remarks:

> Ringgold, who spent a lot of time at this museum looking at the Demoiselles d'Avignon, and looking at Guernica when it was here, absorbing the lessons of Picasso—she's in conversation with him. She is engaging him. Obviously she deals with a whole other set of issues as well,

> around race and the fraught politics of the '60s. But I think linking them together creates a different way to see Picasso.[4]

In fact, what emerges almost instantly are the formal similarities within the two works: the odalisque pose of the woman anchoring the center of each work, the entry of an additional subject in Picasso—on the right, a suggested exit from one of Ringgold's subjects on the left, fragmented bands of color in Picasso, more geometric differentiations and delineations in Ringgold. Disappointingly, the two works, in fact, generate far more dynamism because of these formal similarities, thereby marginalizing Ringgold's work further through contrasting representations of two primal urges. Sex—or violence?

The Picasso–Ringgold pairing has certainly been one of the most often discussed. Helen Molesworth, writing in *Artforum*, describes the pairing as "soft," before suggesting, provocatively, "the gallery feels like a ghost of the old MoMA story: you know, the one about swaggering men making triumphant pictures that change the course of history." Molesworth continues, suggesting that Ringgold's conceptual and contextual astuteness, rendered in full in the work, are more than powerful enough to be made "iconic." "This picture could for sure handle it. Can MoMA? Can we?"[5]

Who knows? Much of MoMA's audience may have a preexisting bias because of the "mere-exposure effect" or the "familiarity principle." Here, familiarity breeds content—people are measurably more responsive to stimuli to which they are more frequently exposed. Given the museum's last major renovation occurred 15 years ago, it is viable that large segments of MoMA's regular museumgoing visitors may initially find the revamped spaces and installations less rewarding.

One of the challenges of this intervention is how to model the artist–audience as a more recent functional transaction between its three participants. Just will this third party, the curator, come into being within the experience? Phenomenology will always already regard seeing and perceiving as exchanges between object and viewer, between the being-in-itself of the object and the being-for-itself of the individual. Where can a curator be positioned within this transaction if it is not conceptually in the gallery where the point of intervention can be made material? By necessity, in mediating the being-in-itself of the object, one Other (a curator) affects the experiences of another Other (a viewer), resulting in a transformed exchange and, by extension, an intervention.

Regardless, the conceptual renovation of MoMA is in its infancy. This initial reinstallation does much to redress the previous predominance of patriarchal, monocultural, modernist artists. Still, these new narratives may exist only temporarily, and continuous reinstallation is planned.

That these newer narrative constructions of modern and contemporary are temporary should surprise no one. This opportunity to recontextualize MoMA's narrative simply mirrors art history's own narrative subjectivity. Lowry outlines the challenge and its inherent shortcoming:

> We did literally hundreds of storyboards about potential installations, because the other thing we've done is move away from thinking that our galleries are purely sequential. Now, each gallery is a self-contained unit linked only by broad chronology, so you can pull one of those units out and put another unit in and it's like substituting one chapter with a different chapter.[6]

The great nonlinear narrative, the jump cut, the postmodern rupture—William Faulkner by way of Quentin Tarantino a quarter of a century too late. These new story lines don't recontextualize artists like Ringgold—instead, they situate them along an expanded periphery. How does Picasso's fetishization of brothel workers align with socially examined violence in modern American cities? What is the link? Alternative contexts of whiteness, blackness, or identity itself could offer a more strident analysis and a more vibrant dialogue. As is, this new juxtaposition merely serves to depict the two cultural crises listed above, with the intimacies of examination buried under the weight of formal analysis.

Regardless of the result, the installation process itself is fraught with hidden power dynamics and transmutations of meaning. The simplest shift—up, down, left, right—can serve to privilege or subjugate a work of art. Linear versus salon style, single image or stacked, wall color. Each situates a work within a curatorially driven context. As Sophie Krzys Acord observes:

> Curators move artworks around during the installation in order to achieve two things: an overall sense of the exhibition as "feeling right" and appropriate relationships between neighboring pieces. This decision-making process blurs considerations of the symbolic meanings of particular artworks and their aesthetic properties. In particular, unexpected physical or aesthetic associations between artworks provide materials for curators to "latch onto" (cf. DeNora 2000) to build their conception of an installation as satisfactory and whole. These emergent cognitive resources were described by curators as "moments of clarity," "little tricks," or "happy accidents."[7]

These "happy accidents" align with another of Acord's findings: the concept of an intuitive response to artworks within a specific space, leading "intuition" during its installation to produce "surprise."[8]

Acord, quoting David Sylvester, makes two other significant pronouncements: one, that the most important individuals within the cultural world are curators, and two, that their rise has been fueled by an "increased importance of mediating between institutional bureaucracy, market forces, artistic representation, and public taste."[9] This may reveal the curator as a chimera of the artworld: a cultural constructor with the capacity to situate economy, taste, and bureaucracy—with agency, but no authorship. This becomes objective without result, a space in which the absent overwhelms the apparent. At MoMA, there are almost 200,000 works in the collection; 89,000 are online, and approximately 2,500 are on display.

Yet, within the controlled confines of the institution, there are fewer opportunities to exercise authorship—and boundless potentialities for autonomous curatorial intervention. As the plethora of recent museum reinstallations suggest, the subjectivities of narrative and history offer as many frameworks for reinterpretation as there are curators. Two limits exist: the scope of an institution's collection and the administration's willingness to construct newer, potentially historically divergent narratives.

This discourse is not new. As early as 2011, the journal *On Curating* published an issue dedicated to the interrogation of curators working with collections. Titled "Reinterpreting Collections," the issue's editor, Marjatta Hölz, differentiated between "participation—the execution of participatory and democratic practices in museum collections," and "interventions—differences in the curatorial of artists, and that of museum curators." In fact, a key problem with the term *intervention* is that it is both a creative and constructive principle. One might argue that interventions are creative because artists offer dynamic perspectives drawn from the poetics of creative practices, while curators are constructive to the extent that they utilize the creative work of others to construct variable and varying narratives. While Hölz refers to both Andy Warhol and Fred Wilson as artists who utilized the encyclopedic qualities of collections to construct alternative meanings—Warhol, through insisting on the exhibition of every shoe in the Rhode Island School of Design's collection, Wilson through the dynamic juxtapositions exemplified in *Mining the Museum*—both are distanced not from the process of creative (artistic) intervention, but from the manifestation of constructive (curatorial) intervention.

The reason? While each of these exhibitions is celebrated as a defining moment of curatorial intervention, in fact each stemmed from a transference—rather than reposition the institution internally, through the lens of self-reflexive critique, in both *Raid the Icebox* and *Mining the Museum*, the power was displaced onto artists as curators. These temporary shifts—at the time—did not represent an institutional change, but instead a contextual and critical transference that reveals structural issues from without, illustrated from within.

Today, Warhol and Wilson are as known for *Raid the Icebox* and *Mining the Museum*, respectively, as Joseph Kosuth is for his 1990 museum intervention, *The Play of the Unmentionable*—approximately 100 works chosen from the Brooklyn Museum's permanent collection, supplemented by texts Kosuth selected. In each instance, these constructions are today artworks that form part of the artist's *oeuvre*, rather than museum exhibitions curated by a contemporary artist. Again, interventions by artists-as-curators are structurally different to curatorial intervention. These former types of institutional critique are both proactive and reactive—proactive to the extent that they indicate opportunities and mirror critical cultural issues and reactive to the extent that artists must be invited to engage in these complex dialogues before these interventions may occur.

Curatorial intervention is entirely different. It stakes a position as gatekeeper, as the sentinel in Franz Kafka's *Before the Law*: "If it tempts you so much, try it in spite of my prohibition. But take note: I am powerful. And I am only the most lowly gatekeeper. But from room to room stand gatekeepers, each more powerful than the other. I can't endure even one glimpse of the third."[10] In fact, this "third" could be read as the metaphorical manifestation of the curator, as their emergence within the artist–audience exchange. Kafka's first gatekeeper is powerful, and each subsequent one more so. This power operates both with and against intention as the figure of the curator works their way through their myriad manifestations. Szeemann chronicles these: "Sometimes he is the servant, sometimes the assistant, sometimes he gives artists ideas of how to present their work; in group shows he's the coordinator, in thematic shows, the inventor. But the most important thing about curating is to do it with enthusiasm and love—with a little obsessiveness."[11] This tendency toward obsessiveness is shared by the artists. As the anonymous interviewee observed:

> In the end it's your work, so what are you going to do? You're not going to let it go forward. I mean, you say, "Yes, I'll do it. Sure, it's a survey show; I want to do it," but then these things unfold. As the process goes on, it becomes clearer and clearer over time how much you're going to have to do if it's not going to fall in a heap.[12]

The strategic alignment here orbits interventionality. The fulcrum is the degree to which curators remove themselves or, to the contrary, envision themselves as collaborators. While in no way connected institutionally or curatorially with the experience described above, Blair French remarked, "we produce a lot of solo artist exhibitions, where—I think, necessarily therefore—the curator will always somehow (in the public imagination, no matter what the reality has been) shadow the artist, rather than lead the artist. So, I think that's quite positive, [and it is] the way in which the place is conceived. But, the fact that we're a museum of and for living artists immediately means that we have a very active, dynamic personality and consciousness to be working with" (Blair French, interview with the author, 2015).

The anonymous artist recognized that the curator's intention was to situate her work within a wider exhibition context based on its location rather than to mediate it through the content of the work itself—rather than constructing the experiential as self-critical or self-reflexive. When asked why she had not addressed the issue of site further and more directly if she felt that her work had not been installed as she had intended, she responded that she would not be "mollified" by a curator taking responsibility for a decision contrary to her own artistic intentions, nor would it make her feel "any bit better."[13] She remarked that she understood the circumstances surrounding the curator's decision, but given its opposition to her intention, it still falls within the ambit of intervention.

Ross T. Smith drew distinctions between interventionist decisions driven by thematic concerns and those driven by functional or material concerns. When describing the circumstances surrounding the reduction of images included in an exhibition that had traveled overseas, he recounted this experience:

> SMITH: [The exhibition] was reduced when it went to London, because the space that was available couldn't hold thirty 1-metre-square images. They really wanted the show, but the gallery wasn't big enough. So, it was cut back to about eighteen or twenty images; I can't remember. And I think also at the [next venue] it was slightly reduced, because of space as well. But this was a long time ago; I don't remember. And it wasn't to do with the images; it was just a space issue.
>
> LEVINE: Okay, so who did the culling of the images?
>
> SMITH: I did—and the curator or director of the galleries, I think.
>
> LEVINE: So, you worked consultatively?
>
> SMITH: Yes.[14]

This is the same artist who had the "mustard yellow" wall experience. Repeatedly, he was experiencing significant decisions that influenced the ways audiences experienced his work. As these two examples indicate, curatorial intervention in Smith's experience oscillated between neutral and negative. Where it operated neutrally, it also resulted from a higher level of artist–curator collaboration and consultation; where the outcome and implications were negative, there was no consultation.

Bayeté Ross Smith, a mid-career artist with an international practice and reputation, holds similar concerns regarding the relationships between the physical installation of works and its constructions of meaning. He related numerous instances over the course of his career during which his work was mediated or subjected to curatorial intervention. He described a specific instance in which his work was recontextualized and marginalized specifically through its installation and presentation:

ROSS SMITH: I was doing the *Our Kind of People* series, which is the head shots of people with the same lighting, same facial expression, different clothing, based on the clothing that they all own. . . . And they wanted to blend them together, and I didn't really like how that turned out. I let them do it, because I was like, "Alright, I'll see how this looks," even though I wasn't that into it. But then what added to it was the way they contextualized the write-up in their materials. It just didn't really get to the heart of what I was attempting to do with that series. . . . So everyone brings . . . a certain response to a certain face and a certain outfit. And I think they made it more into an examination of race, which is definitely part of it, but that depends on who you are; there's definitely a different examination of race, depending on your race. And so it also kind of felt like they were taking a very mainstream, white approach to it, which was fine, but they didn't contextualize it like, "We or I"—whoever was writing that—"see it this way, because this is my background." They kind of made it into what I was saying was how it impacted them, and I didn't really like that.

LEVINE: Had there been discussions around the context of the work?

ROSS SMITH: I had conversations with them, but they didn't send me the text for approval first, so that was something where I was just like, "Okay, I need to make sure I get approval of the text first." That wasn't something where I was, like, really, really angry, but I was like, "You know, I really wish we would've had a conversation about this."[15]

Each of these occurrences was marked by disparities between transparency and agency. And, in both, Ross Smith regarded the power relationship as having been skewed in favor of the curator. In the first example, there is greater transparency, as the exchange was collaborative and, to some extent, shared agency. In the second example, while there was an illusion of transparency—Ross Smith perceived that consultation had occurred and would continue to occur—in fact, decisions contrary to his intentions were being made without his input. Here, agency had transferred wholly to the curator.

Terry Urbahn related an experience in which curatorial intervention would have altered the meaning of an existing work contrary to its original intention. The artist—a mid-career New Zealand artist with an extensive international exhibition history—had been invited by an institutionally affiliated practitioner to participate in an exhibition with a focused, curatorially driven exhibition theme. The curator's stated intention was to recontextualize one of the artist's existing works into the frame of the new exhibition. As Urbahn explained:

> There wasn't any opportunity to reconfigure the work or re-present it, so it all of a sudden got a little bit uninteresting. And she was also wanting to overemphasize that little bit in that one artwork as more of a global theme of mine. So she wanted to exaggerate how much I used the influence of spell-making or whatever in my work, even in the ritualistic way of making the work; you know, sort of trying to make me out as some sort of shaman or warlock or something like that. And I sort of said, "No, no, you're going over the top with this." So it sort of got to a point where I said, "Oh no, I can't come up with any new ideas around this theme," so I didn't take part in that show.[16]

He then went on to narrate a subtler experience of curatorial intervention in which a commercial space had once encouraged him to make more marketable work:

> Every time I had an exhibition with them, I always got a sense that [they were] challenged by my work, in terms of, "How the hell am I going to sell this shit?" So as a dealer, [they] were kind of trying to encourage me to be a little more commercially minded, but I was pretty staunch on that.[17]

These experiences mark what might be considered some conceivable limits of curatorial practice: in one, a curator encourages an artist to consider recontextualizing an existing work—or to simply make new work—which would easily fit within their predetermined curatorial framework. In another, a curator (or gallerist) encourages an artist to alter both the materiality and the context of their work so it can more readily become a part of the system of economic exchange. Neither of these examples is artistically driven. Instead, these are curatorially driven frames within which creative activity would be situated. Similar experiences were reported by Ronnie Van Hout, who recounted an exchange during which a curator informed him that his own description of a work's meaning was incorrect. With a mix of humor and irony, he remarked, "I remember there were many times you'd go, 'I think this work is about this'—you'd be talking about your own work—and they'd go, 'No, no. That's not it. That's not what it's about.'"[18]

Describing the problematics of this dynamic further, Van Hout noted, "curators are between the artists and the work—so they give context and interpret its meaning."[19] Van Hout seems reconciled with this seeming duality, wholly focused on intellectual and creative production, detached, at least at arm's length, from intervention.

Both Urbahn and Van Hout have experienced attempts to mediate their works. If one combines their experiences with the observations of Ross Smith, then one may begin to see the constructs of curatorial intervention emerging. Starting with requesting changes to works, then engaging in the recontextualization of works, and, more problematically, inferring that a creative practitioner themselves is not clear about the meaning of a work of art, each example solidifies the construction of curatorial intervention as an active, mediating practice. This perception is reinforced when considering another instance relayed by Ross Smith in which a colleague was asked to alter a key component of a work. He explained:

> There definitely are ways that the people organizing exhibits—the curators—try and get you to shift things in a certain way. I've never dealt with anything where it completely compromised the work, but I know people who have received really odd requests.[20]

Artists relate, and relate to, their experiences with curatorial intervention in varying ways. The New Zealand artist Stella Brennan meshes creativity with curatorial practice, at times simultaneously—meaning that she must also, potentially, intend and intervene. In one of her earliest curatorial projects, *Nostalgia for the Future*, at Artspace, Auckland, she shared the gallery's exhibition spaces with other candidates for their MFA degrees. Robert Leonard describes how Brennan "rescued" a signature Guy Ngan sculpture—a classic work of New Zealand high modernism—from a post office basement, where it had languished for more than a decade. Of her curatorial practice, Leonard observed that Brennan is conflicted about "coolness," suggesting that, whereas Walter Benjamin tracks the path of an object from contemporary through abject to vintage, in fact Brennan's curatorial and creative practices intermesh each, holding out against "recuperation" at the same time that she confronts its seductions.[21] Elvis Richardson explores similar issues, particularly the seduction of the visual–nostalgic. Operations of curatorial intervention—and its subsequent rectifications—can displace or even mitigate perceptions of positive, neutral, or negative experiential impacts.

Mark Kessell, a New York photographer who first trained and specialized in daguerreotypes before turning his attention to large-scale images, recounted having had an exhibition threatened with cancellation—before a selection of its component works were recontextualized after the show's theme was modified. He explained:

> [The curator] didn't pick anything that they thought might get them into hot water. So, it was a culled show—put it that way. It wasn't merely curated; it was culled.[22]

Having received a letter outlining the need to alter the scope of his project, Kessell responded:

> While I understand the Dean's concerns and the pressures upon [them], I must nevertheless state, quite unequivocally, that I am both surprised and disappointed by [their] decision. From your comments about the Dean's courageous actions in previous situations involving controversial art, I can only speculate upon the reasons for [their] current approach. For [the] university, an educational institution widely

> considered among the best in the world, a university which positively teems with Nobel Prize winners and other minds of international repute, this attitude is, to say the least, unfortunate and regrettable.
>
> I understand that you are in an awkward position, having tried in good faith, to curate an intellectually and visually stimulating exhibition which would offer students and visitors to the school an extended understanding of the human condition. Rather than trying to curtail your efforts the school should applaud them. You have done everything I could wish to champion this exhibition in its original form. I can think of nothing you could do that you have not already done with professionalism and complete integrity. Thank you for trying so very hard![23]

What emerges is a distinction between creative and consumptive agency, the latter being the processes of works that find themselves within the public sphere, ready to be experienced. Whereas creative agency resides wholly with the artist and, to a lesser degree, with curators, consumptive agency is subject to curatorial agency and operation, particularly within the sphere of the gallery or museum.

As a result, complex dynamics between issues of transparency, agency, and power become even more nuanced: not only must one situate the issues of transparency and power within their respective modules, but one must also attempt to parse agency relative to where it might best be situated. Furthermore, this distinction between these two types of agencies means that a curator might in fact assert their power relative to one but not the other, or both—creative and consumptive—against the artist. So, when one begins to evaluate the intersections of these two competing agencies, one must map each issue against its own specific variables and then plot each against the other to determine what would be points overlayed on a graph—in that moment, one would find the intersections between creative and consumptive agencies. Artworks, available for reception deflected to their point of intervention.

In certain instances, artists perceive that curatorial transparency, coupled with shared agency, can have positive impacts on their works. For example, Carlos Rolon, a mid-career artist of Puerto Rican descent based in the United States, believes that curatorial intervention can and should enhance the creation, completion, and experience of visual art. Once, in the midst of working on a new series, he had a fortuitous exchange with a curator. As he explains, she was excited by the works, but perceived there were opportunities to enhance them further: "You're making these paintings, and they're exciting in how they deal with abstract expressionism and action painting. But quit being so insular. Why is everything square? Why not take out a chunk on the left, or a piece in the center? Make a wall relief!" As Rolon explains, he responded, "Damn, you're right. We don't have to leave it that way."

This tendency to stray from a focus on control with the appearance of spontaneity would have been difficult for Rolon. Known early in his career as Dzine, he moved from bulbous hand-drawn and delicately painted graffiti works to DJ booths speeding through the waters off Miami in a cigarette boat for Art Basel Miami Beach. Rolon is a unique combination of prankster-meets-professional, a passion for combining sports with professionalism that leads to some very culturally specific works. The fact that, as a Latinx artist, Rolon celebrates his Puerto Rican heritage, which simply adds to the complexity of his influences.

When asked how he regarded the role of curatorial intervention within the larger framework of his creative practice, he stated that he regarded it as an integral component of creativity, remarking succinctly, "I'm very much open to the ideas of collaboration. I believe that a good curator will make the show and will make my work stronger. I truly believe that."[24]

However, while in certain instances, artists view the collaborative relationship they have developed with curators positively, in others, the agency and power relationships are viewed as being more problematic. In certain situations, artists are even reticent to engage in actions, processes, or practices that are directly requested by curators even if those same actions are to fulfill an artist's stated intentions. Australian artist Elvis Richardson spoke of just such a circumstance:

> RICHARDSON: I was in a show with quite a young curator, and she just didn't involve me in the process at all. Even when I suggested I'd come down for the installation, she just didn't seem to want me there. And then when I got there and I saw the work, she'd put a really tiny screen on quite a big arm that came off the wall, so it looked kind of like a postage stamp on a huge, big, boom. It was wrong, and I was horrified.
>
> LEVINE: That someone didn't want to engage with you, and in the end, made a series of installation decisions that affected the work—and your perceptions and intentions for it?
>
> RICHARDSON: Well, the following day, after the opening, we went and bought another arm and replaced it. I just said, "I'm sorry, I can't have it like that."
>
> LEVINE: So, you changed the work after the opening?
>
> RICHARDSON: Yes, which is always bad; you just feel like it's bad form all around.
>
> LEVINE: So, was she aware that her actions had affected both the content and context of your work?

RICHARDSON: I think she understood the importance. I just had to insist, once and firmly.[25]

Both of the above examples illustrate that the significance of an intervention is not simply a matter of recognizing its existence. In fact, its presence or absence is the least problematic issue that can be illustrated. When artists share narratives concerning the impact of curatorial interventions, particularly if their stories differentiate between impacts on meaning, method, or medium, those impacts can be evaluated to determine if they have fundamentally altered the structure or function of the work or project in question. If not, one might then argue that intervention was of little, or no, significance. If, in fact, it was to be found to be of material impact, then one would have to determine at which variable the intervention in fact operated, and to what extent the intervention represented a collaboration, a compromise, or a command.

Certain examples evidence that, even within the framework of curatorial intervention, its applications vary, with differing effects. In the instances where artists feel that their agency is most usurped, such as the experiences described by Ross T. Smith and Mark Kessell, the subsequent impacts upon intended meaning or envisioned intention are most evident. As Smith remarked, "the curators have the ultimate decision, because it's their gallery. . . . The curators are in control of the artists, and if you want to show, you do what they say, that's it."[26] This notion of functional, structural, and ideological ruptures between curator and artist is regularly echoed within curatorial theory. Yet Smith asserted something else entirely, postulating that the power dynamics and structural relationships result in intentionality being ancillary to both authorship and curator interventionality regardless of content or context. He reinforced this perception through relaying a second exhibition experience in which both the intentionality and the contextualization of the project were altered by and through the exhibition's presentation. In his words:

> They didn't have the right lighting. There weren't enough, and they weren't adequate. They were doing general illumination—they weren't focused on each of the images. And so some of the works were in darkness, and some were in light. And, I designed paint colors for the walls for each show. It was a licorice green, so the room was already very dark. On that sort of background, each image has to have individual lighting to bring it off the background—and then it looked amazing. So, I remember being very disappointed in that show, because it just looked okay—not great—and I couldn't do anything.[27]

Smith described two instances in which the contexts of the *Hokianga* project were altered. In the first, he was actively engaged in the process; to the best of his recollection, he was involved in both refining the selection of the images to be exhibited, although he regarded the ultimate decision to have remained with the curator as a result of institutional responsibilities and the disparities in artist–institutional power relationships. In the latter, the exhibition suffered because it was altered from its original context due to an exhibition design decision, effectively altering viewers' capacities to engage with the works the way the artist had intended. In the artist's opinion, this resulted in an exhibition that "looked okay, but it just didn't look great," and for which the artist was powerless to make any correction—or to inform audiences in any way.

Here, consider Jauss's concept and construction of a "horizon of expectations"—a potential that artworks possess that can be evaluated by how effectively the aesthetic experience, the effect of viewing a work of art, impacts upon or influences audiences.[28] In both instances Smith recounted, the horizon of expectations was obscured: in the first instance, the horizon was partially obscured as a result of his separation from the final selection of images. So the degree to which the works could influence audiences was mitigated by physical distance; in the latter, the works themselves were fully obscured by a lack of light. In this sense, then, the work became wholly invisible in its visibility, for it already lacked the capacity to be seen how the artist intended: it could be viewed as it should have because the exhibition space lacked the capacity to display it in the proper manner. Therefore, artists—not viewers—must situate themselves incredibly low on the horizon of expectations.

Works of art may also be obscured in their entirety simply by not being displayed. Kessell recounted an experience that illustrates this directly, discussing an instance in which he was directed to select a body of work separate from the one he had been contractually invited to display:

> LEVINE: Were you willing to explore the idea of an image-by-image evaluation, or did you just take the approach that your works would be seen as a body of work? And you, as the artist, had made the selection, in consultation with the curator—and it was that or nothing?
>
> KESSELL: Well, I wasn't really given that choice. I'd like to say I was given that choice, and had I been given that choice, I might very well have rejected it on the basis that this particular series is very much intended to hang together as a series; it's not—individual images are not the point. . . . I was simply told, "This show cannot go up. You either change the show or you don't have a show."[29]

Kessell's imagery is not what one would describe as warm or soft. He bridges the aesthetic with the scientific. A medical doctor by training, today he trains his lens on issues of mortality and temporality as well as other significant questions that impact humans as a species. His *Perfect Specimens* series mapped the human life cycle. Full disclosure: he photographed my grandmother for the series, although she is represented in anything but a traditional portrait. He has photographed a series exploring how sight-impaired children navigate a vision-focused world. And he makes no pretensions about his works. While he did explore a more formal sense of portraiture early in his career, this simply meant that he often captured his subjects above the shoulders, to at least give a suggestion of a face. The fact that he did so with one of the most complex and challenging photographic methods—daguerreotypes—meant that even these more traditional approaches were marked by time and chance. As Kessell's account reveals, he was not offered an opportunity to alter the exhibition's original content or to consider whether he would be willing to continue to offer alternative images from the same series. Instead, he was compelled to alter the exhibition in its entirety—basically, to substitute one series for another.

For both Smith and Kessell, curatorial agency had displaced artistic intentionality—resulting in curatorial interventionality. And, in each instance, the artists perceived themselves as subjugated to curators within the power relationship. Despite suggestions that they alter artworks or their components—as both Brad Buckley and Carlos Rolon were—artists may still perceive the overall power relationships that exist with curators to be as equitable as they are disparate. When the general is separated from the specific, artists' reactions to theoretical requests to alter or amend artworks may represent a dialogue as much as it magnifies a *potentially* disparate power relationship as a marked shift. In practice, while artists may see the exchange as collaborative, its opacity still operates to push the differentiations in agency toward opposite ends of the power spectrum.

Finally, in certain instances—such as those shared by Bayeté Ross Smith and Elvis Richardson—the artists perceived that the dynamics and dialogues surrounding the exhibition were congruent with a perception that decisions that impacted their respective exhibitions would be made either personally or in collaboration with the curator. In actuality, each was functionally severed from installation decisions, meaning that alternative interpretations and narratives were able to emerge despite prior discussions with the exhibition's curators.

When this occurs outside the frame of the artist's intentionality, one may encounter experiences like those recounted in relation to a show installed in our anonymous artist's absence:

> ARTIST: I'd only seen the gallery once, and it was hard to figure out how this work would go into that space and make sense. In the end, I just said to them, "You're going to have to figure it out, because I'm not here, I can't do it. Just do your best," and then they did a couple of things that I thought were terrible. They double-hung works that were never supposed to be hung that way. It looked okay, but conceptually

it was a travesty as far as I was concerned. But it was done; it was on the wall. If I'd been there, it wouldn't have happened.

LEVINE: And was there any indication in the exhibition that any of the decisions that had been made about the installation had been made by any member of the exhibitions, curatorial, or administrative teams?

ARTIST: No. You know that that doesn't happen.[30]

The artist was caught in a physical manifestation of what should have been a conceptual and creative challenge—how does one best approach a body of work that physically seems to exceed a venue's capacity? At times, artists welcome curators to share agency, but the execution and realization of curatorial agency may manifest itself *against* their visions, interests, and intentions. In such cases, both the relational and actual positions of artist and curator oscillate—yet, while the artist may be a curator, despite assertions to the contrary, the curator may never be the artist. And, while there has always been the potential to critically situate curatorial intervention within an artist-curator dialectic, rather than one of artist-viewer, this construct would alter the very nature of creative and curatorial exchange.

NOTES

1. Goldstein, "So, Is MoMA Woke Now? Not Quite."
2. Schjeldahl, "The Exuberance of MoMA's Expansion."
3. Reilly, "MoMA's Revisionism Is Piecemeal and Problem-Filled: Feminist Art Historian Maura Reilly on the Museum's Rehang."
4. Goldstein, "So, Is MoMA Woke Now? Not Quite."
5. Molesworth, "The Kids Are Always Alright: Helen Molesworth on the Reinstallation of MoMA's Permanent Collection."
6. Goldstein, "So, Is MoMA Woke Now? Not Quite."
7. Acord, "Beyond the Head: The Practical Work of Curating Contemporary Art."
8. Ibid., 454.

> "For most of the curators I spoke with, the installation was the most 'passionate' part of the exhibition-making process: only in the space of the gallery can you understand how 'everything works.' Curators described this as a 'magical' process, involving 'intuition' and 'surprise.' They regularly said, 'I know it when I see it.' Statements like these (and, more importantly, the actions they represent) denote the importance of the embodied mastery of the 'codes' and 'conventions' which order artistic production and mediation. These tacit practices, articulated in video-elicitation interviews, revealed a variety of conventions for installing an exhibition of contemporary art: mix wall-mounted works with sculptures to provide a pleasing assortment of media, position particular artworks together to bring out planned similarities, install particular 'key' artworks in prominent places, and make the space as a whole look clean and inviting. This sense of 'feel-

ing right' is not known, however, but is rather achieved through the situated practices of moving things around and 'giving them the eye.'"

9. Ibid.
10. Kafka, "Before the Law."
11. Obrist, *A Brief History of Curating*, 99.
12. Anonymous artist, interview with the author, December 14, 2015.
13. Ibid.
14. Ross T. Smith, interview with the author, February 28, 2016.
15. Bayeté Ross Smith, interview with the author, September 18, 2015.
16. Terry Urbahn, interview with the author, November 3, 2015.
17. Ibid.
18. Ronnie Van Hout, interview with the author, August 27, 2015.
19. Ibid.
20. Bayeté Ross Smith, interview with the author, September 18, 2015.
21. Leonard, "Stella Brennan: History Curator."
22. Mark Kessell, interview with the author, Part 1, October 15, 2015.
23. Kessell, correspondence provided to the author.
24. Carlos Rolon/Dzine, interview with the author, December 15, 2015.
25. Elvis Richardson, interview with the author, July 26, 2016.
26. Ross T. Smith, interview with the author, February 28, 2016.
27. Ibid.
28. Wlad Glozich, Introduction, in Jauss 1982b, xii.
29. Mark Kessell, interview with the author, Part 2, October 31, 2015.
30. Anonymous artist, interview with the author, December 14, 2015.

FIVE

The Work Is (Not) on the Wall

In 1975, the Australian artist Domenico de Clario installed a work at the National Gallery of Victoria—complete with a fully functioning electric radiator adjacent to a full can of kerosene. What other response could the curators and conservators have? The work was removed.[1] This countervention against curatorial intentionality and authorial agency—combined with administrative structures that control how cultural venues engage with audiences—suggests that, for as long as curators have been exhibiting art, they have been the pivot point between institution, artist, and audience. This could, at times, compel curators operating within institutional roles, or to request that artists alter their works, but a more collaborative initial framework is structured to prevent these later renegotiations.

Conflicts between agency, transparency, and responsibility situate curators in a conundrum. Where does their primary obligation reside? Is it to artists, with a concomitant responsibility to ensure the most unfettered access to the museum or gallery as a site for dialogue, discourse, and exchange? And does that obligation extend to a responsibility to artists that their works be presented without extraneous contextualization or interpretation? Or is it more pragmatic? Does their primarily responsibility lie with the institution?

Part of the problem derives from a shift in the praxis of curatorship itself—from the archive to the expository or from curator to the curatorial. As Maria Lind observed in differentiating between these two constructs, "the curatorial is akin to the methodology of artists focused on the postproduction approach."[2] At its core, Lind's "postproduction" approach becomes, essentially, the strategies of the postmodern: fragmentation, collage, montage, multiple perspectives, issues of originality and authorship. Lind suggests that the curatorial situates curators as authors in part because of the authorship inherent in exhibition production and narrative construction. Perhaps an equally significant question concerns the ways in which this authorship extends to objects. Here, the term *object* still means, as Heidegger theorized, something that still contains meaning and value—in essence, the object still contains the capacity to convey. When drained of this ability, object becomes thing. And an art object is not merely, contrary to linguistic turns, simply an objet d'art. Heidegger's object is a being-in-itself, fully realized. The art object should occupy this same space and have its significance attached thereto. Instead, through curatorial intervention, and the curatorial, the object, the being-for-itself, becomes subjective, unmoored. The art object is beyond the artist. It is discrete—and fragmentary—to the extent that its meaning as object may exist separately from its exchange. Instead, its meaning exists phenomenologically, which allows for its consideration beyond the authorial narrative. It is constructed, but not bounded, by its physical objectness nor is it by necessity confined to the artist-object story. This multiplicity, which arises in part because of the art object's existence as being for itself, is what allows its transfiguration into alternative narratives. Its meaning is, essentially, elastic—and separate from the artist's intentions. This interpretive malleability is what allows curatorial intervention to displace artistic intention. The former is speculative, while the latter, presumably, didactic. Recall Robert Leonard's observations from chapter 3. There, he remarked on the elasticity, within certain limits, that curatorial practice and exhibition can offer—apart from installing works specifically contrary to artists' intentions, that is, upside-down.

Apparently, the aversion to installing works upside down is common among museum curators and directors. In a 2010 interview for *On Curating*, Jean Hubert Martin spoke of the 1999 collection reinstallation at the Museum Kunst Palast of Düsseldorf. Having invited two artists to reinstall the permanent collection according to their vision, Martin issued a single prohibition: "we had an agreement not to allow little jokes with the artworks, like for instance to hang paintings upside-down." Unsurprisingly, this caveat is not always successful. In 1961—despite curators' best efforts I am sure—Henri Matisse's *Le Bateau* was installed upside down at the Museum of Modern Art, where for 47 days it was viewed—by a total of more than 60,000 museumgoers—before stockbroker Genevieve Habert, an astute visitor who had seen the show more than once, identified the installation error. Upon bringing the matter to the attention of a museum guard, he is reported to have curtly responded, "you don't know what's up and you don't know what's down and neither do we."[3]

Just as curiously, Jackson Pollock's painting *Number 27, 1950*, also has a history of being installed based on curatorial interpretation—and, this time perhaps more significantly—prior to exhibition documentation. A 2015 Artnet.com article describes the painting, then on display in the Whitney Museum's inaugural exhibition for its westside space, as being installed "the wrong way."[4] Drawing on the work's limited exhibition history prior to acquisition, as well as both a previous, similarly oriented installation at the museum and documentation from Pollock's 1950 exhibition at the Betty Parson Gallery—the only documentation of the work installed during the artist's lifetime—the museum was confident with their decision. As Dana Miller, former Richard DeMartini Family curator and director of the collection at the Whitney Museum, remarked, "I've heard that the vertical hang at Betty Parsons was due to space limitations, but I haven't seen any documentation to support that. Space was perhaps a factor, but if Pollock had objected to it being hung vertically, it wouldn't have happened."[5]

So, while there might be a tendency to ascribe a hierarchy to Leonard's early curatorial practice—curatorial autonomy contra artistic intentionality, in fact what was at stake was the opportunity for unfettered intellectual inquiry. This may well have prioritized curatorial intervention, but it also illustrated the inherent dynamics and tension between intention and intervention. Aaron Seeto, director of Museum MACAN, addresses the problems that too narrow an emphasis on the intention/intervention dialectic can create. As he explains:

> These types of interventions are happening all the time, but they're just probably more nuanced. When I have taught students focusing on curatorial studies in the past, I always identified that there are many, many different types of curators. You could be working for a private collector, with a really narrow understanding of what they're interested in; you could be a curator working for an auction house; or, in a public institution or an independent space. And, these situations have different historical contexts and demand what I would call different ethical approaches. It's not necessarily a question of whether one is being more or less interventionist; it's a question of what are the ethical boundaries. And those ethical boundaries, I think, are determined by the broader cultural, political, and social contexts which surround each of those individual spaces.[6]

Both Leonard's and Seeto's experiences illustrate how curatorial intervention is as much a strategy as it is an experience. Each suggests that reinterpreting works within defined conceptual and contextual frameworks allows curators to construct dialogues beyond those initially envisioned by the artist. In fact, both Leonard and Seeto regard the opportunity to interpret works in innovative, new ways, is one curators should explore. As Seeto explains:

> As a director, I was quite interventionist—while also understanding that I wasn't an artist. My role as a curator was to really try and push the meanings of works in different ways. Or, to play the role as a commissioner—find pots of money for artists. It was an opportunity for us to really look at what an artist may have been dreaming about but not necessarily had the opportunity to fully conceptualize, or never

> had the money to produce. So, I think the roles of the director, the commissioner, and the curator are quite interesting. And, each necessitates a type of intervention.[7]

A conundrum emerges. In response to an initial set of questions for our interview, Seeto described the more formal, institutional model of curating as "old-fashioned," suggesting instead that issues surrounding curatorial intervention are better situated within discussions concerning cultural, social, and political contexts. At the same time, he has described both his curatorial practice and his approach as an arts administrator as "quite interventionist"—to the extent that, by taking the initiative to engage with artists and explore the limitations of their projects, there may well be opportunities for more expansive works and more preeminent results. In many ways, Seeto and Leonard are the antitheses to a type of curator chronicled in Linda Weintraub's "Curator(i)al Flow Patterns":

> Conventionally, curators have served as stabilizing forces by centralizing their authority and pursuing precise directives, thereby assuring a predictable result. As in ecosystems, these principles are optimal to accomplish a task within a stable environment that has a pre-determined goal. Curators subscribe to this principle when they organize exhibitions that are held in closed environments in which interaction between the artist, the artwork, the audience, and the environment are suppressed to accord with the sterilized austerity of museum protocols and the authoritarian determinations of curatorial mandates. Such separationist tactics are characterized by the hidden artist, the anonymous curator, the mute audience, and the neutral site.[8]

At times, the anonymity of "the curatorial" can be favorable. Artist and curator Ruark Lewis, senior curator at a nonobjective art space in Sydney, Australia, describes the innate power in operating outside well-established exhibition frameworks within a diversifying museum. As he recounts, "I started making programs for the Art Gallery of New South Wales in about 1985. In those days, Australia was just moving into a contemporary art format in the museums and the art galleries." He continued, "Theory hadn't entered the academy until about 1985 in Australia. Art history was taught, and at a certain point there was a shift to postmodern theory. A very radical one, too. It happened almost overnight. The fashion changed so quickly it was tangible before me, which I thought was very odd but interesting. In music and performance—particularly in music—you know theory is a given. But not for something like architecture and the visual arts—at that stage."[9]

Suparak explains how the collaborative nature of artist–curator dialogues and discussions can at times facilitate better outcomes for both the artists and the respective curatorial project. While definitionally interventionist, this discursive give-and-take should not automatically be viewed as suspect or problematic. Suparak has shared how, in certain circumstances, she may ask artists to alter or edit elements of a larger video or moving-image project to meet the exhibition's intent or, in others, to adhere to the scope of the opportunity available (as in a time-specified exhibition submission). She explains:

> [w]hen I was curating film events, there were many instances in which I showed an artist's looping video installation. If I was showing the work in a sit-down screening, I would ask for an excerpt and write in the program notes or on the title card for the video "excerpt" or "excerpts."[10]

As one of the most nuanced contemporary curators working today, Suparak is extraordinarily knowledgeable regarding strategies that can best promote and protect artists' creative interests. Pragmatically, she works to ensure that her practice exercises collaborative agency rather than interventionality.

New Zealand arts administrator and chief executive officer of the Museum of New Zealand Te Papa Tongarewa, Courtney Johnston, shares similar concerns regarding how curatorial strategies can be positioned institutionally. When asked, while director of The Dowse, if curatorial imperatives for situating a critical art–historical dialogue as part of the institution's objectives were codified, Johnston remarked, "It's more values and culture. If you think of values as being almost unchangeable, and culture the way that values are expressed over time in a changing manner, I think that's a model that fits quite well."[11] Perhaps this emphasis on transparency is prevalent in New Zealand, as Walker also shares a similar perspective. He offers, "I think that as long [as interventions] are driven by clear values, like better outcomes for artists, better outcomes for audiences, better outcomes for curatorial development, opening up greater spaces to think and move within, then that should remove the fear. But I think that what everyone thinks is that it is a compromise or a diminishment."[12]

In the examples above, curatorial intervention operated within established and delineated parameters. On every occasion, curators and administrators regarded interventions as an opportunity to offer unique opportunities for artists and to generate relevant discourses for constituent communities. For Johnston, this meant situating curatorial practice specifically within an ethical frame with a culturally responsive focus; for Leonard, this involved examining the potential dialogues that could be created through different approaches to specific objects; for Seeto, intervention and negotiation arose from the understanding that the artist had the potential, if desired, to create an even more multifaceted project that could resonate with more diverse audiences across a greater number of locations. Any visible absence of intervention that exists—not through absence, or lack, but by choice—can suggest that artist–curator negotiations and dialogues have been transparent and balanced. Such an approach can predominantly establish negotiated frameworks and ensure that in-process projects will not produce unintended consequences, misunderstandings, or misinterpretations regarding aims and objectives.

At times, as Astria Suparak highlighted, curatorial intervention can offer opportunities to better contextualize works within defined parameters, which could involve subject, duration, or construction.

Both Justin Hoover and Megan Tamati-Quennell, each with extensive experience working in community-focused exhibition spaces, describe differing approaches to audience and context. In part, Tamati-Quennell's framework is bounded by Te Tiriti o Waitangi, the Treaty of Waitangi, which works to facilitate a bicultural frame for representation for both the indigenous Māori and Pākēha (those of European descent) in Aotearoa, New Zealand. Hoover's curatorial identity emphasizes internationalism and the unique negotiations that occur therein. As Hoover explains:

> Most people believe that museums are spaces where only final products by professional people can have space to be displayed. At the [museum], we don't believe that. We believe that anybody can make anything and share it with each other, as long as it has a story and it has meaning to them. . . . [W]e believe that that leads to bonding, bridging, and empowerment, and that makes our community stronger.[13]

He then positioned his frame for curatorial intervention using principles that he described as being inspired by the Fluxus movement, remarking that "Fluxus was very interventionist a lot of times, so while there was a lot of back story, like, you know, 'These people are doctors; they're doing this project.' You don't necessarily need to know that; you just can get a sense of it."[14] He prefers projects to develop organically and then for information to be shared as necessary. When asked about his willingness to reveal these specific operations or to share curatorial interventions within the scope of a specific project, the exchange was as follows:

> LEVINE: How much of this type of behind the scenes pre-planning or pre-production work—and that's probably the word to use—how much of that information might be shared with an audience, if any?
>
> HOOVER: I think it depends on the context. If we were able to set up an artist's or curator's talk, I would share whatever people wanted to ask me about. I probably wouldn't advertise it in public, on wall labels, or in marketing.

Tamati-Quennell regards curatorial intervention as generating two problems that impact directly upon transparency and agency: one, that curatorial intervention misstates artists' intentions, and two, that curatorial intervention has the potential to serve only the needs of curators—particularly when living artists do not have opportunities to participate in dialogues. As she remarked:

> I don't shoehorn artists into my ideas. I'm not saying I don't have any agency, but my ideas come out mostly through the artists' works—and out of my respect for them.[15]

Regardless of the level of each variable's transparency, curatorial intervention is always situated by agency and power. The pure economics and political economies of curatorial intervention manifest differentially depending upon motivation and outcome. For our purposes, the term *political economy* refers to the specific qualities and concerns to curating, particularly those outlined in chapter 1 by Anton Vidokle. If we return his drivers for curatorial intervention, each is situated by a collapsing distinction between "political economy" and "economy."[16] Curatorial intervention oscillates between, and blurs the boundaries and distinctions among, distinct economic differentiations. At times—as Justin Hoover does when he contrasts economic benefit with curatorial intent—curators construct their exhibition frameworks to address issues surrounding pure economy. Quite literally, the economic value of art can overcome challenges generated by its content. Narratives that address this issue can then evolve to include even more subtle discussions of political economy, as contextualized by the intricacies of Vidokle's and others' thinking.

The potential to site curatorial intervention as a predominant concern—in contrast to evaluating it purely as the manifestation of agency—emerges here as a result of the intricacies explored in the opportunities Hoover recounts. Speaking about working within an international context, he explained how the pure economy of exhibition can at times be used to cloak, or even shield, a project's more subtle meanings, and how these lures of economic value and exchange can manifest as a type of smoke and mirror that may obscure the more radical content that an exhibition contains. As he explains:

> I put together a group of artists from North America, both female or transexual identifying. These artists use the body to struggle against heteronormative values. At that time, serendipitously, a gallery in Tehran asked if I would curate a show for them. So, I said, "Sure, let's do a video show, so I don't have to ship anything." I proposed nine videos—knowing that three would be censored for sure, and hoping to get six through. They were six super-wild videos. So, I presented this show in Iran. Then, Shanghai is a little bit more flexible, because China—unless you're overtly talking about the Party—doesn't really care so much.[17]

By stating that "the foil of capitalism was used in my favor this time," Hoover exposed a fundamental conceptual schism between curatorial intentionality and economic reality. He used the power of global financial exchange—literally, the perceived power of the dollar—to mitigate the problematics of artistic intentionality. He then overlaid his intentionality on the project, stating, "I proposed nine videos, I censored three." Hoover grasped that, by asserting the notion of pure economic value, he could likely overcome any censorship issues. This finding illustrates curatorial intervention as an operational mode of pure economy.

Any emphasis on visitor and viewer experience becomes key to a holistic approach to curatorial intervention. As Megan Tamati-Quennell, curator of contemporary Maori art at the Museum of New Zealand Te Papa Tongarewa, observes, questions of curatorial intervention may also emerge through a necessity to address disparate perceptions of cultural concerns within curatorial practice—and institutions. Speaking of one of the earliest exhibitions of contemporary Maori art at Te Papa, Tamati-Quennell explains:

> I curated a show which was probably the first major survey of Ngāi Tahu art and taonga. And so, it was huge as it traversed hundreds of years of settlement and development. For the exhibition, I worked with 10 Ngai Tahu iwi kaumātua [tribal elders] whose role was to support me in my role as the exhibition curator and to bind the Papatipu runaka communities they came from. The project worked conceptually with the idea that, if Maori are unique culturally within the world and Ngai Tahu are unique within Maori, what were the concepts or signifiers that exemplified Ngai Tahu as a culture and as a people. We worked through that idea and in the end those concepts or signifiers were distilled down to four main themes or ideas. The Iwi (tribe) were clear they wanted to be presented within the exhibition within the present and the future, not just the past, as is often done. The four concepts the show worked with translated in English as culture, tenacity, sustainability, and innovation, which I interpreted as cultural characteristics of the tribe both past and within modernity. There were subthemes within the four, but all the taonga and art sat within those four main ideas conceptually. I remember undertaking an early presentation of the exhibition conceptually at Te Papa to the programming team, and one of the programming team said to me, "But those concepts or ideas could be related to any culture," which seemed a curious thing to say. My response was to say, "Well, we're a part of the human race, aren't we?" What I was really trying to express with that and within the show was our humanity and how we are not so dissimilar to other people.[18]

Tamati-Quennell planned to utilize the existing organizational and structural systems that operated within her institution, to leverage them for the artistic community and to work with tribal elders to construct an exhibition marked by cultural, creative, and artistic significance, excellence, and symbolism. At the same time, she recognized that to do so she would also have to negotiate any possible preexisting institutional prejudices. Through her curatorial agency, working collaboratively with tribal elders, she constructed an exhibition narrative that situated the works of indigenous New Zealanders within a wider cultural context, thereby placing them within the more complex curatorial and cultural dialogues that existed within the museum. At the same time, the specific issues of curatorial transparency and agency remained opaque, and the question of curatorial power remained difficult to situate. Of concern in this instance is the existence of cultural power that is not transferrable—quite simply, there are issues that attach to the specificities of agency within Maori culture that could not have been ceded or acquired, regardless of where she was situated within the wider museum frame. What is imperative to remember in this context is the understanding that artists, curators, and administrators do not—and cannot—approach the process of intervention, or any of its variables, other than subjectively apart from when such interventions are driven institutionally.

When this occurs, many curators can find themselves trapped in a bind, mediating between artists and administrators—through a potential veil of intervention. The alternatives? Consultation and negotiation.

These strategies mirror those utilized by Tamati-Quennell in relation to her curatorial and collaborative processes for the Ngai Tahu exhibition. Potentially, any single instance of curatorial intervention can be defined within several frames, whether that of the exercise or operation of curatorial power, the operation of pure economics, the problematics of political economy, or the historicity of institutional hierarchy. What binds these functions together is that each is an operation of curatorial intervention itself—meaning each shares some quality of mediating the artist–audience exchange, while not being visible as a mediating event operating between the intentionality and reception of art objects or experiences.

That curators find themselves in this theoretical predicament might come as little surprise since one may argue that their role has shifted from keeper and creator to mediator and manufacturer or from keeping objects and exploring interpretations to mediating between constituents and manufacturing meanings. This is most evident in the exchange narrated by Morris, in which she was not only able to thwart an administratively driven curatorial intervention but was also able to ensure that the artist remained connected to the intentionalities that were outlined when the project had begun. Having been encouraged, though not required, to place a restricted-content warning at the beginning of the exhibition, the curator declined to do so—much to the artist's disappointment:

> MORRIS: I didn't put the note on the door. And the artist was actually kind of like [clicks fingers], "Oh, darn. I wanted you to put the note on the door."
>
> LEVINE: Oh, interesting.

MORRIS: Because she runs towards any kind of controversy. Or I guess she thought that it would draw attention. And I said, "I appreciate that, but I don't want that kind of attention, because that's not part of our intent with this show." I mean, men would put on these costumes, and then they'd say things like, "This is heavy." And to me, that's what it was about, and I felt that if we put that note on the door, and then someone walked in in black leather [clicks fingers], boom; of course, they're going to immediately think—but there was never a problem.[19]

Situationally, curators may determine the limits of their interventionist practice, as Morris does in this instance, while Seeto describes how independent curators may have the flexibility to consider and reflect a far wider scope of practices than they perhaps could within an institutional frame. And, within an institutional frame, a curator might engage in a form of curatorial intervention that alters a fundamental, core component of institutional practice—such as a collection—if it were deemed to not fully reflect the community with which it is supposed to engage. He remarked:

> What's kind of interesting is that, and I'm talking outside of the institution, but I'm looking at other institutions in this instance, no one questions the types of narrative trajectories in established collections. So, no one talks about whether there's an interventionist role in the development of Australian collections, or international collections, or nineteenth-century collections in museums. But when you're talking about things that have maybe a closer alignment to the types of politics that emerge from communities or from non-dominant groups, then there's always an issue.[20]

Consequently, it can be difficult to determine the implications of curatorial intervention, as it operates both within and against established frames. Suparak, for example, also having worked independently and institutionally, attempts to bridge the gaps between existing/traditional and interventionist practices in varying ways. She reported requesting edits of film, digital, and moving-image works for specific projects as and where appropriate. This approach derives, in part, from her perception that at times artists do not necessarily produce works that function equally well across all projects. As Suparak described:

> Sometimes, artists would send me works in progress, and I think that probably in those cases, I felt more comfortable asking for a particular kind of edit—like if they were looking for feedback or just wanted me to know what they were working on, in case it worked for a future project of mine. . . . As for other kinds of edits, off the top of my head, I can't think of a specific example. But I think there must have been a time in which I thought maybe a section was—maybe the pacing was not great; maybe it was very slow for a screening context.[21]

Suparak described having fewer hesitations offering suggestions or engaging in dialogues when a work in progress was being presented; a work that was completed and had been exhibited previously presented its own unique challenges.

> LEVINE: Is there scope within the framework of this type of [interventionist] practice, or are there ways in which this information might be shared with an audience? Is there a way to say, "This unique structure, a collaborative design between the gallery and the artist, dot, dot, dot"? Or is that something that might never appear, just because it's too—it's either not significant, or it's too problematic?
>
> SUPARAK: How have I framed it publicly or in written format?
>
> LEVINE: Yes.
>
> SUPARAK: I think I've usually buried or kind of glossed over how much production or hands-on work I was doing, because that might take the focus away from the artist, or be seen as controversial—and of course, again, it would only happen with the artist's consent.[22]

Suparak acknowledges the problematics of intervention, particularly the extent to which a curator's role becomes apparent, illuminating the reality that, for the sake of the work's reception, she often "buried or glossed over" her dialogues and contributions. While this appears to be the foundational moment in interventionist practice—to the extent that action (or lack thereof)—may or may not be distinguished by the artist; in fact, in the moment of negotiated intervention, it is the distinction between authorship and agency that teeters. Viewed from the artist's perspective, this same issue is an inherent problem in curatorially driven collaboration. Do artworks by necessity become collaborative when they are curated? Are artists simply subjects, or artworks components? Leonard, Hoover, and Tamati-Quennell address "collaboration" specifically in their interviews, although the concerns surrounding the issue remained apparent.

For Seeto, collaboration is a dialogic process. He recounted an instance in which he suggested to an artist that the project the artist had proposed was limiting—that it merely adhered to existing codes of exhibition and display—and that there were alternative, more engaging, more community-based, and more dynamic ways in which the artist could proceed. He explained their process:

> I said to him I really don't understand it, you're coming to a contemporary art organization, you're asking me to put these objects under a glass case, it doesn't make any sense. I love the work, but to present them in the way you're proposing would be to really limit what is

> really beautiful about them. I asked him, "Wouldn't it be more interesting if we actually had dinner with these things?" He had made this massive dinner service. He went away and thought about it. And, it was the beginning of one of his very important series of projects. He orchestrated beautiful meals, in strangers' homes, eating off his ceramics.[23]

Yet, when asked specifically about the implications of his engagement with the artist, Seeto revealed two facts: one, that stories of this collaborative process had been made public on many occasions, and two, "it's not a relationship of co-author. I'm not a co-author of this work."[24] Despite engaging in a constructive process that enhanced the project's outcome, Seeto did not regard his involvement as amounting to authorship in any way.

So, from the curator's perspective, are the impacts of intervention measurable? And how should curators perceive the potential implications of their engagements with these works?

Arguably, a significant difference exists between perceptions relative to curatorial interventions that are individually motivated and those that are initiated at the behest of other individuals. That through proper planning, dialogue, and consultation, the need for subsequent curatorial intervention can be mitigated. What occurs, in this example, is essentially an a priori curatorially driven, positive-outcome intervention. The intervention is driven by the curator and powered by individual agency. Interventions motivated by or stemming from individual curatorial agency often appear to produce positive outcomes, particularly in the narratives of impacted artists and curators. As the example shared by Tamati-Quennell illustrates, intervention can be grounded not in personal preference, but from community responsibility and concern.

On the other hand, when institutional administrators, trustees, or other interested parties—including the viewing public—are the impetus for curatorial intervention, perceptions and outcomes differ.

NOTES

1. Marshall, "Ghosts in the Machine: The Artistic Intervention as a Site of Museum Collaboration-Accommodation in Recent Curatorial Practice," 65–66.
2. Stainforth and Thompson, "Curatorial 'Translations': The Case of Marcel Duchamp's Green Box," 240.
3. Cascone, "This Day in History: The Museum of Modern Art Hung a Matisse Upside Down and No One Noticed."
4. Boucher, "Whitney Museum Hangs Jackson Pollock Painting the Wrong Way."
5. Ibid.
6. Aaron Seeto, interview with the author, March 17, 2016.
7. Ibid.
8. Linda Weintraub (2013). "Curatorial Flow Patterns." Reprinted at lindaweintraub.com. http://lindaweintraub.com/curatorial-flow-patterns/.
9. Ruark Lewis, interview with the author, August 17, 2015.

10. Astria Suparak, interview with the author, October 16, 2015.
11. Courtney Johnston, interview with the author, June 30, 2015.
12. Tim Walker, interview with the author, August 24, 2015.
13. Hoover, interview with the author, August 11, 2015.
14. Ibid.
15. Megan Tamati-Quennell, interview with the author, February 7, 2016.
16. Vidokle, "Art without Market, Art without Education: Political Economy of Art."
17. Hoover, interview with the author, August 11, 2015.
18. Megan Tamati-Quennell, interview with the author, February 7, 2016.
19. Shannon Morris, interview with the author, May 18, 2016.
20. Aaron Seeto, interview with the author, March 17, 2016.
21. Astria Suparak, interview with the author, 2015.
22. Ibid.
23. Aaron Seeto, interview with the author, March 17, 2016.
24. Ibid.

SIX

Intervention Contra Engagement

In the early 1990s, Andres Serrano traveled to the University of Alabama at Birmingham as a visiting artist. Private donations funded the purchase of one of his photographs, *Pieta II*. The image shows a plastic model of Michelangelo's *Pieta* immersed in cow's blood and urine. Immediately, the work sparked an uproar in conservative Alabama. Viewers who wished to see the work, which was temporarily displayed in the rear of two spaces at the university's ground-floor Visual Arts Gallery in the Humanities Building, had to sign a visitor logbook. Contrary to popular misconception and urban myth, the university had not purchased a *Piss Christ*.

From mid-2001 until late 2011, I was director of the Visual Arts Gallery. Sometime in 2010, the phone rang one afternoon. "Hello?" A voice responded: "Hello. This is Andres Serrano." A discussion ensued. Serrano had heard that the university had difficulty exhibiting its work, which he too understood to be a Piss Christ, and wanted to offer the possibility of making available works from alternate series that might be more accessible for Alabama audiences. I paused. What might those be? To this day, I understand the university to still hold *Pieta II* in its collection—and am still unaware of its having been publicly exhibited. Like many of the works included in Joseph Kosuth's exhibition at the Brooklyn Museum, *Play of the Unmentionable*, Serrano's photograph, exists in a lacuna: too valuable—monetarily, conceptually, and programmatically—to deaccession, too important to simply store, too controversial to exhibit.

In 2006, I curated an exhibition that comprised the body of works currently completed by New York artist Lee Brozgol for his *Hidden America* series. Of the more than 30 gouache paintings, a small number addressed specifically adult themes, including nudity. Since the gallery space was utilized by the university for other purposes, I was asked one day to remove six of the works on display in advance of a university recruiting event. Prior to installing the exhibition, I had acquiesced and excluded one work, which could have been viewed as the most problematic—to the extent that a drawing suggestive of BDSM (bondage, domination, submission, and masochism) could be deemed so—from the exhibition. Given the subject matter of the works now in question—nudes—coupled with the fact that each was a gouache painting as opposed to a conceivably more explicit image, such as a photograph, I declined.

The following Monday, I arrived at the gallery to find—at first glance—nothing to indicate that the six disputed works had been removed and reinstalled. But something seemed out of place. Later that morning, after walking the exhibition and examining every work closely, there it was. Each painting had some signifier—often a very clear referent—that could be read to determine the state the correspondent represented. North Carolina was in the wrong place. Yes, the "objectionable" works had been removed—and reinstalled incorrectly.

This was a revelation: in a single instant, intervention subsumed content. There was no direct correlation between a specific work and its anchor. Instead, each work was equal in absence. No nudes was good news. The issue centered specifically on nudity, not on context. Each work was reduced to a trope, valued identically and, apparently, valueless at the same time—at least for whoever moved them.

This conflation of general with specific occurs far more regularly than one might imagine. At times, administrative intervention can and does address complex issues of racial, gender, and sexual inequities—as the University of Alabama at Birmingham's medical school did with the removal of the Marshall Bouldin III painting, *Medical Giants of Alabama*—which included a depiction of 19th-century gynecologist J. Marion Sims, among others—from the university's Center for Advanced Medical Studies. The painting also depicts the then-enslaved Anarcha Westcott, who endured multiple surgeries by Sims.[1] In 2018, a J. Marion Sims statue, located in New York City's Central Park for 80 years, was also removed.[2] In each of these instances, the decision maker determining the removal was neither a curator nor a museum administrator. For the UAB painting, a commission of doctors made the decision; for the statue, the New York City Design Commission made the decision. But, in many instances, curators and administrators clash over the implications of certain works, and their significance for exhibitions and institutions. Nudity may be fine at a distance—but at eye level, 60 inches above the floor, apparently not so much.

Equally as important, the contextual and conceptual rhythms created within the curatorial process are often easily ruptured. The process of experiencing a work of art outside its curatorial and conceptual narratives redefines the result. Debra Diamond, curator at the National Museum of Asian Art, recently observed:

> You can put two artworks together—what do they say, a painting is worth a thousand words? Well, you can put two paintings together and they can be worth a hundred thousand words, like they can sing when you put them together. Or they can be inert. Or they can actually fight with one another, too. So I want to make sure our combinations sing.[3]

To more fully situate intervention's operation in this context, it is imperative to consider two divergent positions. One, the curator–administrator relationship. How does structural hierarchy impact the efficacy and operation of curatorial intervention? Is curatorial intervention primarily a top-down or bottom-up structural response within a specific institutional frame. Two, how should the artist-curator-administrator-institution relationship be dissected to analyze this seemingly linear, structural relationship? Does hierarchy curtail the operation of curatorial intervention? While the two-party curator–administrator dualism mirrors its four-element artist–curator–administrator–institution structure, they do not necessarily operate in parallel.

Contemporary writing on the artist–curator relationship suggests a close correlation between curators who encourage artists to explore or extend their capacity to create and the potential for administrators to have to intervene in some fashion—whether positively or negatively—to the extent that the National Coalition Against Censorship compiles an "Art and Culture Censorship Timeline."[4] While not every event chronicled reflects a curator–administrator difference, each that does suggest that, when administrators direct curators to take specific actions, there tends to be a problematic, and often interventionist, outcome. In these instances, differences in perspective regarding transparency, agency, and power become significant. The dynamics of curator–administrator exchanges raise several issues. One, how do administrators mediate differences of intentionality between artists and curators. Two, should administrators broker compromises or determine solutions in instances in which the parties are unable to compromise? Three, how nuanced should administrative mediations be? Should administrative decision making also generate interventions that produce meanings outside an artist's intentions, and, if so, how might administrators position or situate their roles in relation to the exhibition's curators?

Whether in the smallest art spaces or the largest cultural institutions, administrators often encourage curatorial intervention if the action will prime a work to further generate critical or cultural discourse. So how are contemporary institutions structured, theoretically and practically, to contextualize curatorial intervention. How an institution is structured, and whether that structure facilitates or thwarts curatorial intervention, depends on the curator's position within the institutional frame. Are they autonomous, for example, or are they subsumed within an organizational hierarchy? Are they the institution's sole—or predominant—curatorial voice, or are they part of a team? These questions emerged in a discussion with Adam Lerner, former director of the Museum of Contemporary Art Denver, who remarked:

> As the curatorial field has expanded, you have an incredible divergence between on the one hand, what young curators are learning in programs of curatorial practice, reading curatorial journals, and, on the other hand, what is actually happening in a lot of museums. And that is partly why—if you talk to many museum directors—they will say it has been really hard to hire a contemporary art curator. The curator and museum director have different expectations about the role. So, I think that there is a real misalignment happening right now with these crazy expectations. There are ten jobs in the world that really embody the kind of theoretical analysis that so many of these journals are exploring. Those are the biennial exhibitions that really create the sort of canvas for a curator to explore ideas through art, and through curatorial practice. And, I just don't feel like that's happening within institutions apart from biennials and those sorts of independent agencies.[5]

One wonders, then, are institutional structures capable of fostering curatorial practices that engage in complex interrogations of contemporary art distinct from, or instead of, curatorial intervention? Can an institutional structure be transparent regarding the artist–curator–institution transaction that would then arrive to the audience defined—if not unmediated? To illustrate these issues, one needs to determine where the interventionist responsibilities lie when a mediated work engages with an audience. Adam Price, co-director of the Sandhills Institute and former director of the Salt Lake Art Center, recounted such an experience when discussing an externally curated exhibition in which the politics of nudity and sexuality had unexpectedly come to the fore:

> It was literally only two days before the exhibition opened when I was in the gallery that I discovered what other images were in this book. It was a disaster, from my perspective, because this was in our main gallery. It was our biggest show, probably of the year, and I had this work in there that was going to just completely destroy any other dialogue that the exhibition might have had the potential to create, as well as potentially impact our funding. And the resolution of this was that we put the work under glass, open to a page that did not have the nudity in there. But the fact that it was under glass meant that the audience had no ability to see the other images of the work. I'm fairly sure that we, at least in the didactic materials, alluded to the images that could not be seen. But I doubt that we did an extended discussion in a way that really would have supported a dialogue about the self-censorship that went on there.[6]

This comment suggests first that the administrator was compelled to make a decision regarding the exhibition contrary to the guest curator's intentions; second, that there was some mention of and attempt to—to the best of the administrator's recollection—contextualize the material that had been censored, but this was not brought to the fore; third, that there was no mention of the fact that the decision to alter the content of the work had been made specifically by the administrator—at least from our conversations—thereby leaving the possibility of the perception that the curator had selected the specific work on view, despite the fact that she had selected an entirely different work, for a range of differing reasons.

Gail Andrews, former R. Hugh Daniel Director of the Birmingham Museum of Art, shared that she once had a curator remove a work that had the potential to generate a multifaceted dialogue around challenging issues in contemporary culture. As she explained:

> A trustee and his spouse came in one Sunday afternoon, and watched the entire video, and spent a lot of time with it. I talked to the curator, and said, "I think this is a great moment to have people in, and to have a conversation about artistic intention and non-intention—to discuss what the piece is about."[7]

Instead, with a week of the exhibition's run remaining, the curator removed the work. The experience is similar to curator Claire Gannaway of the Manchester Art Gallery removing a pre-Raphaelite work—*Hylas and the Nymphs*—to generate dialogues surrounding the exhibition of art. As Ellen Mara de Wachter wrote in *Frieze*, "A curator temporarily removing a painting from a gallery she oversees in order to raise questions about it is not censorship; it's curating. But the questions raised by Boyce's gesture are many and wide-ranging."[8]

While intervention is not synonymous with censorship, their perceptions and correlations are closely intertwined. Instances of censorship still occur so regularly that *Hyperallergic* issues an annual chronicle of censorship—the most recent of which appeared in January 2020.[9]

Yet, strangely, the possibility of these value judgments impacting the processes of reception appear significant even when their operation is less clear. If curators base their assessment on the work's perceived value—communicative or cultural—rather than the artist's intentions, then they have fallen victim to a conundrum first raised by Hans-Georg Gadamer in *Truth and Method*:

> If it is true that a work of art is not, in itself, completable, what is the criterion for appropriate reception and understanding? A creative process randomly and arbitrarily broken off cannot imply anything obligatory. From this it follows that it must be left to the recipient to make something of the work. One way of understanding a work, then, is no less legitimate than another. There is no criterion of appropriate reac-

> tion. Not only does the artist himself possess none—the aesthetics of genius would agree here; every encounter with the work has the rank and rights of a new production. This seems to me an untenable hermeneutic nihilism.[10]

An untenable hermeneutic nihilism. Obviously, this cannot be an intended outcome from experiencing a work of art, but the audience model of art allows for an endless construction of open, subjective, individuated interpretations that are each "legitimate." When a work is removed from an exhibition, curatorial agency contradicts transparency—the removal of the artwork is absolute, yet the reasoning attached thereto may remain opaque. Regardless of reasoning—which can include artistic, cultural, legal, or schedule—its shift toward opacity results in a dual operation of interventionality.

At times, a decision not to intervene administratively may reinforce artistic intention. Andrews shared an experience surrounding the display of Hank Willis Thomas's banner work, *Priceless*, at the time installed on the exterior of the museum. The work depicts the funeral of Willis Thomas's cousin as told through the language of a late-2000s MasterCard ad. "Bullet ¢60. Picking the perfect casket for your son: priceless." Once installed on the façade of the museum, public reactions were charged. The power of the misunderstanding seemed poised to overwhelm the subtleties and truths in Willis Thomas's work. As Andrews related, she received a call from city administration, relaying the responses that were being generated.

> ANDREWS: You have the Black mother of a son who's been slain saying, "What's the museum doing?" It's the only time city leadership has ever called me about an object on view, saying, "I don't know if you're aware of the big poster that's on the outside." And I said, "I know what you're talking about." And, I explained the work to the Mayor's chief of staff, who responded, "Oh, well, that'd probably be fine if we were New York or Atlanta, but a lot of people are asking. They just don't understand what it's about."

Andrews describes how she perceived an opportunity for the city to work closely with their employees to foster better understanding, while considering additional options for improved dialogues. Suggestions that the local newspaper explore the matter in greater depth did not eventuate. Although some perceived the work as one that required a high degree of explanation, Willis Thomas was confident that the power and universality inherent in *Priceless* were timely and self-explanatory.[11]

Priceless so altered the Birmingham community's consciousness that—more than a decade later—its impacts and implications were still resonating. For a 2018 conversation as part of the *Third Space* exhibition project,

Willis Thomas returned to the museum to discuss *Priceless*, this time installed in the museum's foyer.

Administrators must consider the extent to which curators wish to foreground their existing collections as well as the extent to which external forces—trustees, boards, councils, or community pressures—compel them to act in this manner. Courtney Johnston, then director of the Dowse Art Museum and today chief executive of the Museum of New Zealand Te Papa Tongarewa, remarked:

> If you continuously bring in blockbusters, then you are training your audience to only visit you when you bring in a blockbuster. You are not actually using your natural resources—which are your collections and your relationships with artists. If you are spending all your time every two years preparing for a show that you've brought in from the V[ictoria] & A[lbert], or, you're showing something because it will bring in the crowds, why would anyone bother to come see your ceramics collection?[12]

Five years later, during the COVID-19 crisis, Johnston is still leading by example, emphasizing the power of existing resources and the many opportunities collections offer for reinterpretation. Johnston offers an interpretive approach that can reveal the schism existing between curatorial intervention and the politics of expectation. She illustrates the difficulties that can arise when curators prioritize temporary, blockbuster exhibitions in preference to those available internally, and the challenges administrators face when confronted with how to challenge curators to work with artists who can utilize existing museum and gallery resources. Furthermore, Johnston suggests that issues surrounding artists, both how they are conceptually situated within an exhibition framework and where the curator might position them therein, can rely upon willingness from artists to become the "face," as well as the "subject" of an exhibition, explaining that, at times, an institution may "foreground the artist's personality and life as part of the way of understanding their work."

At the same time, Blair French, formerly chief curator at the Museum of Contemporary Art, Sydney, and now director of Carriageworks, discussed circumstances in which institutions challenge curators to practice or intervene in spaces in which they might not be completely comfortable, but within which the museum at large wishes to operate. Having worked within both contemporary art spaces and major public museums, French remarked that:

> We don't require curators to take on a project they're not committed to or enthusiastic about. To do so would be to put the project—and the artists involved—on the back foot from the start. That said, part of my job is to enthuse and be passionate about a wide range of things and to encourage and challenge individual curators to on occasion move beyond their particular strengths, their specialist knowledges and their

> known networks. It benefits their professional practice, and the museum.[13]

This ability to create spaces for curators—as subject matter experts—to engage with complex issues was echoed by many other curators and administrators. Tim Walker, a museum professional, consultant, and arts administrator spoke of how, at several institutions he is familiar with, curators and administrators have intervened within artists' creative processes to offer positive contributions that assist artists with refining their intentions. He shared an experience, focused on intentionality and transparency, that emerged from an artist mentorship program he collaborates with in Aotearoa, New Zealand:

> WALKER: I was sitting with an artist in a cafe in Ponsonby, and I said, "Okay, why do you take your photographs?" And—in a way that was astonishing, because so few people can answer the question—she very quietly said, "I want to make my subjects world famous." And I asked, "So you're saying like New Zealand Idol?" and she said, "Yes." I asked, "So what would happen if we said—on a piece of paper—'Because it's really important to me that my subjects become famous, are there different ways I think about the ways I take photographs?'" And she sat there, and looked and looked at it—and got her iPhone out "Can I take a photo of that?" she asked. The reason I'm saying this is because this isn't the way a curator would normally work. The outcome was that I said to her, "Well, we could sit here and talk about how to think about approaching the MCA," and she held her hand up and said, "You don't need to say it. That would just make me famous, and that's not what I want."
>
> LEVINE: Talking about your project—you were having a conversation which caused her to radically expand her project. Are these types of conversations, or negotiations, or discourses the types of things that should, or could, be shared?
>
> WALKER: I use that example quite often when I'm doing strategic planning with organizations, whether arts organizations or business. I put up a traditional purpose-based model, Disney, which is driven by a purpose focused on happiness. Then, I'll say that this is a better example. What is amazing is that she actually knows what she wants to happen in her world—and that she very quickly worked out that *what* she was doing was never really going to deliver the *why* she was doing it.[14]

Walker's conversations with artists explore variables that can emerge from discussions and negotiations, offering opportunities for intentionality to consolidate within diverse institutional and experiential frames.

His questions situate and address how intention impacts the potential for specific outcomes. His interventions—and for our purposes, Walker serves in multiple roles, and operates within multiple frames—are highly detailed and incredibly nuanced, addressing the specific needs of the artist, and they serve to specifically address and reinforce the original and primary intentionalities of the artist. The interventions stood as manifestations of curatorial transparency that situated the agency with the artist—Walker neither insisted upon nor initiated changes to the project, but the alterations that did occur were the result of conversations focusing specifically on the artist's objectives and intentions. The conversations did not alter the works' meanings or methodology, and, where they did affect the materiality of the project, they did so to enhance and extend engagement rather than reduce or diminish opportunity.

Apart from visual analyses of violence, perhaps the works that garner the most highly charged audience responses involve artworks that represent or imply sex. Kon Guoriotis, former director of the Casula Powerhouse, Sydney, and former head of visual arts at the Australia Council, shared his experiences installing a work by artist Dani Marti that explored the politics of identity and intimacy. He focuses on a discussion between himself, Marti, and Nicholas Tsoutas, the exhibition's curator, regarding a specific element of the project. As Guoriotis explains, "I did ask Dani if the money shot on the masturbating piece could be perhaps darkened a little bit. And Dani said, 'No worries. I know what to do.' So, he was wonderful; he just made it a bit darker. And sure, we did, in a sense, ask Dani to censor his work, but would have put all the work in the exhibition on Dani's work—and there really were 15 other excellent works. And, he was wonderful in that process, because he was not just thinking about his own work, but also the others. And—everyone walked past it."[15]

This collaborative approach was key for both Guoriotis's administrative approach and his expectations regarding how curatorial negotiations should operate in relation to artworks exhibiting at his institution. Guoriotis has also shared that he regards contracts between artists and curators, or artists and institutions, as bilateral: artists should be able to withdraw their works from an exhibition should the institution not fulfill its obligations to them, and institutions should have the expectation that artists will deliver the agreed-upon work on time and on budget. With these caveats in place, he did not generally find a need to intervene within curators' practices from an administrative position or perspective. He did, however, relate other instances from his earlier career as a curator when his practice was the subject of administrative intervention, mediation, or what he regarded as undue influence. He outlines an approach to artist–curator engagement, which, if they adopted universally, would limit curatorial mediation. In his words:

> The role of a curator is to ensure that the initial intention is very clear, and that there are no misunderstandings, either from the organization's or the artist's perspective. Because once we remove this "halo" from around the artist and bring them down to earth, we are a worker and they're a worker, and they're a professional and we're a professional. Then, we're no longer looking with glittering eyes to the skies at this wonderful, hovering artist, we're actually down on the ground, having a discussion.[16]

Somehow, contemporary culture has a neologism for a renowned architect—a starchitect—but the similar notion "startist" remains absent from our contemporary lexicon. Recognizing how integral it is that institutions and artists establish intentionality from the outset, Guoriotis places this responsibility squarely with the curator. He states, categorically, that the curator must ensure that there are no creative or institutional misunderstandings regarding intentionality. Instead, he situates the curatorial role to ensure that artistic intention is clear. This position, this responsibility, must attach to the autonomous curator as a manifestation of curatorial intervention.

Guoriotis also outlines contexts in which audiences, not artworks would be subjected to curatorial intervention. One need only consider a recent controversy at the Saatchi Gallery in which works by SKU, which were deemed offensive to the Islamic community, "should remain on the gallery wall but be covered up with sheets."[17]

Guoriotis shared a similar incident concerning a collaborative project that interrogated aspects of Aboriginal–Pacific Island cultural conflicts within Western Sydney, and the resultant works, some of which had the potential to offend members of the Pacific Island community. Even though the work had been created by a member of the community, it was determined that in the interests of the overall project—which included a cultural component—a physical impediment should keep visitors outside the exhibition galleries until the cultural ceremonies had occurred. As Guoriotis recounted:

> No public access would happen at the beginning of the performance. I was lucky that the gallery had two levels, so we were in the upstairs part. I had security at all entrances saying, "No, we want to focus on the performance," so [I] made no issue about the painting. And then the decision was that the community would be given the right to vacate the performance at the end, and all their people would be able to go, not knowing anything about that painting. And so that's what happened. We then opened the exhibition. And of course, there were some people who stayed behind, and there was some criticism, but we gave everyone forewarning before they actually went up to the gallery, and then they had the option of proceeding or not proceeding. And in the end, the artists were relatively happy with that, and the exhibition just continued without any incident.[18]

Here, both Guoriotis and the curator had intervened in the work prior to its reception. They anticipated potential problems and acted to mitigate them through controlling access, installing signage, and establishing wayfinding—meaning that, as well as delaying the work's debut prior to the community event, they also installed signage as the event ended. Their challenge involved predetermining specific elements that were likely to cause offense; at the same time, it is the most prudent approach to preventing potential issues that may arise because, at face value, visitors and viewers cannot say that they have not been forewarned.

The administrative interviews each reinforced an element of these positions. Individual administrators sought to clarify that curators have a responsibility to define the roles of the parties to the artist–institution exchange as well as to the artist–audience exchange. In certain instances, administrators even admitted that there is scope for some degree of curatorial intervention, such as in instances for which the unfettered exercise of artistic expression within a specific community may knowingly cause outrage or offense from the outset, as part of an artist's intent—with no other significant value or component. As Administrator AD.09 wryly remarked, "it's distasteful, at best, for a curator to say, 'I don't like that shade of blue; could you try something more aqua.' You know, that's just stupid, and a curator who acted like that wouldn't be a curator for very long. But to say, 'Would you mind not putting swastikas in that painting?'—that seems like a different thing."[19] When asked if those types of negotiations should be transparent, he continued, "[t]here's all sorts of compromises that we make, and we're not telling everything to everyone. I think as a general question, we shouldn't hide these negotiations from the public." What emerges is a litmus test for mediation, establishing that in certain instances an interventionist approach may be appropriate, while at other times it is at odds with the fundamental structures of both artistic and curatorial practices. This same position was echoed by Friend, who remarked:

> If the artist comes to me and says, "Look, I'm trying something new; I don't want to do my last series," I'm 99% of the time willing to work with the artist to develop the new project. . . . And there's occasions where that backfires, you know. But it also means that you can be the first place to show that show; you'd be the first place to do that project. It provides agency for the artist. I think it's better for their practice, rather than—and I think it's better for our institution, if we're seen to be showing new works by these artists, rather than being just the latest place to do the same show that everyone else has kind of done.[20]

Often, museum administrators are inclined to allow curators to make exhibition decisions predominantly unhindered and unencumbered, as Gail Andrews did; alternatively, they may suggest a more dialogical approach, as with Adam Lerner; or yet again, they may focus instead on facilitating the artist's engagement with the institution while operating outside it, as with Tim Walker's analytical and situational strategies. In every example, the outcome is an exhibition methodology that attempts to engage artists and audiences despite curatorial intervention—and to preemptively mitigate attempts to refigure these artist–audience outcomes.

Alternatively, in certain instances, administrative intervention can deflect the potential agency of curatorial intervention, specifically when such mediations can more effectively situate curatorial practices within their preestablished parameters. As an example, consider a curatorial project—described by Steven Rand, director of apexart—in which key components of the exhibition were reimagined after grant funding had been received. Rand, and apexart, were left to determine and evaluate the extent to which these proposed alterations would alter the project's initial, overarching goal. Rand described how each proposed change was material—and how difficult it can be at times to convince curators to take the risks necessary to realize a project as it was originally envisioned. As Rand explains, curators can often see benefits through revisions—whether that means originating a touring show in a different location or changing an exhibition's physical structure or architecture. From itinerary to content, from sponsorship to advertising, every decision a curator makes is assessed against their stated intentionality, which may or may not necessarily align with the intentionality of the artist.

Reuben Friend, director of Pataka Porirua in New Zealand, spoke in part about practices that can operate outside traditional constructs of curatorial thinking, and may epitomize much curatorial practice today. Within a conceptually expanded framework, curators become individuals who can extend and enhance the scope and range of artists' capacities or capabilities. And, while Friend recognizes adopting these extended practices may create additional complexities and challenges, but regards the approach as integral to both his administrative expectations as the director of a cultural institution and his curatorial opportunities, which can create enhanced exhibition opportunities for artists. As he explained:

> I feel like a curator is somebody who looks for trends that are happening in the art world and identifies them, and that's their role, to identify those things that are interesting, and then to work with artists or communities to advocate for those communities within the institution. And I think that's great, if the curator can do that. So, they will work with the artist and they'll come to me and they'll come to me and be like, "We need to do this," and I tell him, "Push me really hard, ask me for as much money, even though you know we can't afford it. Go beyond what you know we can actually do. If the artist wants to do something crazy, let's try and do it, because it's your job to convince me that we can do it, and I have to find the money to make these things happen."[21]

Using this interventionist model, Friend's comments reveal four critical curatorial engagements that emerge in the process of exhibition-making: (1) curators identify emerging trends in contemporary art; (2) curators work with artists or communities that can make these trends manifest creatively within the institution; (3) curators encourage artists or communities to propose projects that extend their usual or perceived limits; and (4) curators advocate for the institution's actual capacity to realize the project. At least one of these responsibilities is clearly interventionist—encouraging an artist or a community to propose a project that extends their traditional limits. By and through making such an assertion, Friend acknowledged several key issues, including both that curatorial intervention operates at the institutional level and that it mediates the creative process. While at The Dowse, Te Papa's Courtney Johnston echoed Friend's perception:

> Curators often see part of their role as encouraging artists to extend themselves. Bigger paintings, bigger sculptures, bigger shows. We ask for that occasionally, but one thing I've become increasingly aware of is that when you ask an artist to make anything larger you're potentially asking them to absorb more production costs as well. So, we give grants to buy materials to offset the requests we make.[22]

By recognizing this, Johnston strives to mediate many of the structural and functional issues that can surround curatorial intervention. In fact, while curatorial intervention may be activated by a request, it can be actuated only through the result. And, while the economics of the exchange are agreed, the transparency of the intervention remains opaque. The artist benefits from the institution's mitigating additional challenges and expenses—the problematics of scale and price—but the audience most likely remains unaware that the artist negotiated to work on a larger scale and extend both their concepts and practices. Functionally and structurally, the issues that may have hindered a larger-scale project are resolved; the fundamental philosophical problematics of intervention remain: the artist–curator or artist–institution transaction may well remain unseen.

When administrators or institutions do attempt to mediate works in favor of audiences, it is driven by the assertion that these practices are, in fact, in the audience's best interests. As Blair French explained, while his institution is not in the habit of interfering with artists' works, they will engage in dialogues that involve protecting the public's safety, whether physical or conceptual. He remarked:

> We're not trying to impose some of kind of rigid structure that withholds your [artists'] creativity and your spatial thinking. We're doing something because it's very real, and because the experience of the audience is important; you know, we want them to be able to move through a space in a way that is appropriate for the work. And often an

> artist will intend to make these challenging or tricky or whatever, but we want them, nevertheless, to be able to have an appropriate experience, but we also want to protect your work and your experience. So, it's actually about us mediating that.[23]

Consequently, the first challenge becomes situating the work physically and the ways in which an institution will engage, collaboratively, to achieve this goal. Once the work is positioned, or negotiated, the more complex questions surrounding the problematics of subject matter can emerge. French continued:

> We will, if we've got really, really difficult work, or we anticipate things being difficult or offensive to some people, whether that's nudity, sexual content, language, whatever; we might consider how the work is displayed and placed. It might not be at the—I might suggest it's not the first work that everybody who walks into the gallery sees, et cetera, and maybe a little bit of warning labelling. And a lot of it's around the way in which our hosts host people. We don't have guards; we have hosts. But nothing has been withheld, pulled, altered. And we've had a lot of conversations about where we're going—what that means for us.[24]

In contemporary cultural institutions, issues often emerge surrounding how to site and conceptually situate complex materials. The issue is so nuanced that, in 2008, on her *Museum 2.0* blog, Nina Simon outlined the range of potentially sensitive issues using a scale from "Safe Zone" (including poverty, population growth, and politics) to "No Way" (from hate crimes and the death penalty to religion).[25] These subtle differentiations and the capacity to situate complex and challenging issues within structural or metaphorical frameworks that will not immediately alienate viewers are ideas mirrored in French's statements. For example, he asserts that, in general, the opportunities for artists are not hindered within his institution—either physically or conceptually—by those working at an administrative or a curatorial level. Still, few organizations have formal, written guidelines that direct their institutions administratively or curatorially regarding the display or exhibition of artworks—apart from those put in place by national or international bodies, including Museums Australia, Museums Aotearoa, the American Association of Museums, or the International Council of Museums. In fact, one is more likely to encounter such policies when exhibiting in secondary schools, tertiary education institutions, public sector offices, or related facilities than when working formally with arts-based organizations. To illustrate this point, a Google search for the phrase "guidelines on the display of artwork" returns 800,000 results, while a search for the phrase "guidelines for the display of artwork" returns 801,000 results. In both instances, no nationally or internationally recognized museum, gallery, or exhibitions-based cultural institution returns as one of the top 10 results.

Lawrence Rinder also emphasized that any curator working with an artist has a responsibility to be fully aware of their practice—to the extent that such knowledge should have the capacity to mediate any need for curatorial intervention. Over the course of his interview, he observed:

> Curators go into relationships with artists—or should—with their eyes open. If you hire an artist to do a commission piece, you should know a lot about that artist. You should know what they've done in the past, what they're likely to do in the future. And if there are any questions about what they may do, a conversation up front about expectations I think is totally reasonable. And if the artist does not choose to work within that framework, they're free to walk away. Once a process has begun, however, and an artist is taken on and there is a shared framework of understanding about the outcome, if something happens within that framework that suddenly the curator is not comfortable with, I think then it is problematic to intercede at that point. That's a very general statement—and probably in the specifics, I find exceptions—but I think that is a greyer area to me.[26]

Adam Price suggested that the same approach should be taken toward curators, meaning that institutions should position their curatorial strategies and their institutional messaging in such a manner that the need for curators to intervene in artists' projects, or the need for administrators to direct curators to do so or not, is mitigated. Speaking of the third major institution he had directed, he commented:

> Social practice I think is requiring a stronger role and participation from the curators to help coordinate the activity that needs to go on. There's really a way in which I think people who are very ego-driven—and who might, in some other life, have been artists themselves—have become curators. And the risk for me, from an institutional perspective, is that the entire institution becomes about the curator, rather than about the artwork. And that's a problem I've run into with some frequency. And so, for me, trying to harness the energy of the curator, both to serve the purposes of art and to serve the purposes of the institution, is a constant challenge, essentially.[27]

In a time in which social and economic revelations, such as investing in prison phone systems or tear gas manufacturers revealing the same cultural connections that Hans Haacke illustrated in his *Shapolsky et al. Manhattan Real Estate Holdings* in 1971, administrators are cautious. While few of the senior-level museum professionals interviewed shared specific instances of curatorial intervention, each offered insights regarding the specific challenges that can arise when artistic expression must be balanced with institutional image or resolve. However these exchanges emerge, if at all, each represents a complex negation between artist, curator, institution, and audience. Suggestions, alterations, amendations—each is an indexical and lexical map of the elasticity between the parties.

As important, the degree of curatorial intervention being driven by administrators varies based on perceived outcomes or consequences: in Guoriotis's example, the goal was to soften challenging imagery without impacting content or context. The outcome was achieved. In Tim Walker's example, the intervention resulted in a markedly enriched project, with elements that had not originally been components of the artist's work. At the same time, the impetus and agency for these enhancements rested with the artist. With Andrews, the curator removed the work in question from the exhibition—unintentionally an operation of curatorial intervention with a work that was scheduled to be rotated shortly thereafter. For Rinder, the outcome required recognition and negotiation; and, for Friend, the impetus for curatorial intervention was the opportunity for curators to extend, and enhance, their artists' projects beyond what had initially been agreed to, and intended.

These outcomes establish that it is the opacity of curatorial intervention, rather than its operation, that is particularly problematic for administrators. Given the potential outcomes, it is imperative to situate curatorial interventions within a framework bounded by variations of transparency, agency, and power.

Within reasonable limits, administrators anticipate curatorial intervention, which may provide valuable opportunities for creative and constructive dialogues and may extend the range or scope of artists' projects. As well, curatorial intervention may encourage professional development.

These dialogues can both reflect institutional intentions and address the diverse needs of audiences. When administrative decision making impacts upon curatorial practice, causing or instigating curatorial intervention, establishing responsibility and agency can be difficult.

As significant, curatorial interventions that are motivated by or driven administratively may operate with, alongside, or against *curatorial* intentionality as well as *artistic* intentionality. In certain instances, as in each of Gail Andrews's examples, curator intervention would have limited further dialogue—although each with radically differing outcomes. In the example narrated by Guoriotis's narrative, the edited video work, curatorial intervention's agency and transparency lay with the curator, with the power remaining with the artist. The impacts and outcomes were positive. Still, each of the above interventions remain largely invisible to audiences. While questions of transparency and agency may oscillate between administrator and curator, intervention—curatorial agency—generally remains opaque to audiences.

Clearly, then, both administrative decision making and the administrative frame issues alter the outcomes of curatorial intervention. As these examples illustrate, curatorial intervention can be driven by, and mediated positively or negatively through administrative decisions and institutional opportunity. Regardless, the synthetic operation of curatorial agency remains largely unaffected.

NOTES

1. Vedantam, "Remembering Anarcha, Lucy, and Betsey: The Mothers of Modern Gynecology."
2. Sayej, "J Marion Sims: Controversial Statue Taken Down but Debate Still Rages."
3. Mitchell, "A Smithsonian Curator Opens Up about Artwork and How Her Own Work Has Changed during the Pandemic."
4. National Coalition Against Censorship, "Art and Culture Censorship Timeline."
5. Adam Lerner, interview with the author, 2015.
6. Adam Price, interview with the author, 2015.
7. Gail Andrews, interview with the author, May 20, 2016.
8. Mara de Wachter, "After the Nymphs Painting Backlash: Is Curatorial Activism a Right or an Obligation?" She continues, "Does it matter whether the decision to remove the work was made by an artist or by a curator? How might the public be involved in deciding and creating new meaning of what is shown? How do we manage the revisionism of white- and male-dominated art historical canons? And how can museums best communicate with their publics when it comes to activist programming devised to alter the status quo?"
9. Batycka, "Art and Creative Acts That Were Censored in 2019."
10. Gadamer, *Truth and Method*, loc. 2172.
11. Gail Andrews, interview with the author, May 20, 2016.
12. Johnston, interview with the author, 2015.
13. Blair French, interview with the author, August 20, 2015.
14. Tim Walker, interview with the author, 2015.
15. Kon Guoriotis, interview with the author, September 3, 2015.
16. Ibid.
17. Waterson, "Saatchi Gallery Covers Up Artworks after Muslim Visitors' Complaints."
18. Kon Guoriotis, interview with the author, September 3, 2015.
19. Lawrence Rinder, interview with the author, April 4, 2016.
20. Reuben Friend, interview with the author, March 24, 2016.
21. Ibid.
22. Johnston, interview with the author, 2015.
23. Blair French, interview with the author, August 20, 2015.
24. Ibid.
25. Simon, "Self-Censorship for Museum Professionals."
26. Lawrence Rinder, interview with the author, April 4, 2016.
27. Adam Price, interview with the author, September 29, 2015.

SEVEN

Intervention Today

This book grew from a two-decade interrogation into how curators impact the artist–audience exchange as well as the reasons the dynamic between three congruent parties seemed to be opaque. Given my background as a curator and critic of contemporary art and culture, most narratives used to illustrate key points have been drawn from the visual arts. The concepts and constructs may well apply to curatorial practices in encyclopedic museums, or they may be better suited to the examination of interventionist practices in contemporary institutions and kunsthalles.

What is clear is that interventionist practices are not solely limited. The practice emerges across kunsthalles, contemporary museums and galleries, and encyclopedic institutions. At the same time, parallel institutions may be more structurally adaptable regarding exhibition narratives, particularly when historical work is being contextualized. I am reminded of observations by the distinguished and highly awarded history curator Richard Rabinowitz, formerly of the New York Historical Society. A passionate advocate for the narrative potential of objects, Rabinowitz is well known for his capacity to make static objects spring to life. Of the many lessons Rabinowitz has embodied over the course of his distinguished career, few are as prescient, or as transformational, as his concise synopsis of a curator's responsibilities. As Steven Lubar observes, for Rabinowitz:

> There is no "sharp line separating the 'object' itself from the interpretive and physical interventions made by curators and designers." You use objects because they are "sticky things . . . meanings adhere to them." "Meanings adhere to them," but they don't tell stories, in themselves. That's the curator's job.[1]

If one were to substitute artwork for objects, curatorial intervention would seem distilled into a single paragraph. Replete with curatorial intentionality, and operating with artworks replete with meaning, curatorial intervention emerges as the "job," as the responsibility to display and interpret objects, to assign and critique meanings, and to construct engaging narratives that viewers find accessible and informative.

None of these opportunities can operate within the dualistic and dialectical frame of reception theory. We must be beyond issues of absolute intention and unfettered reception. Instead, the curator has emerged, somewhat problematically, at the site of this exchange with the responsibility to situate and reveal their agency. Still, the art and history curators will diverge, as one constructs with a view of immediacy, while the other interprets against the specter of history. Either way, curatorial intervention operates, and its impacts upon intentionality and reception evolve.

Perhaps the most significant development in the immediate future will be the impact of diversity and inclusion upon histories of intervention and potential alternative strategies. Issues surrounding key 21st-century responsibilities—including addressing the power disparities identified by the #metoo movement as well as those structural imbalances that systemic bias and racism have perpetuated—can radically transform curatorial practice for the future. As significant as these strategies will be, neither these nor any other revaluation of curatorial practice will adapt and transcend without first acknowledging that the presuppositions upon which many artistic exchanges are built—intentionality and reception—are already deflected by the operation of curatorial intervention, with its opacity, agency, and power.

Curator-driven collaborations that can explore these issues will be crucial to fomenting institutional and structural change. Most importantly, a more comprehensive narrative surrounding the operations of curatorial intervention may provide audiences with opportunities to consider alternative experiential outcomes. Simply knowing the extent to which a creative project is realized is as imperative a contribution to knowledge and analysis as the mere appearance of a work within a gallery or museum.

I have always believed that it is both the role and the responsibility of curators to make their thematics and constructs as transparent as possible. This does not mean sacrificing the quality or concept of an exhibition. Instead, this construct requires curators to acknowledge the multilayered approaches diverse audiences bring to their individualized encounters with art. In the early 2000s, while working as a university gallery director, I came to the realization that a standard trope of "curator-speak" is both encyclopedic and evasive simultaneously. When asked by a visitor to explain a work, I responded, "It can be read on a variety of levels." That work could, and every work can. Knowing that Kehinde

Wiley's *Napoleon Leading the Army over the Alps* references Jacques-Louis David's *Napoleon Crossing the Alps* serves to better contextualize Wiley's painting, but for some viewers that information may have no immediate, direct resonance. The question curators and museums must answer is how best should this correlation be conveyed? Or should it be conveyed at all? Clearly, moving forward, the responsibilities to inform and entertain will be more crucial than before. Just as a quarter-century ago, the emergence of poststructural and postmodern curatorial and exhibition practices allowed the physical manifestation of critical historical narratives through then-contemporary artworks. Creative in intention, curatorial in its interventionality, the postmodern exhibition represented the apex of critical art installation. Today, those very same strategies have been reappropriated by artists. When curators deflect their intentionality in the service of an alternative narrative or experience, intentionality exceeds its authority. There is a need to draw back the curtain on opportunities to turn artworks on themselves or to extend their meanings in the service of philosophical dialogues beyond their scope. There is, clearly, the opportunity to address the shortcomings of reception theory and to insert in its stead a new model: intervention theory. Grounded in the intentionality of artists, the interventionality of curators, and the reception by audiences, this new model would serve to make meaning more manifest.

Making these meanings manifest may well be the sine qua non of curating—the capacity to transform works from intention to manifestation. While there is no specific imperative to do so, there is a professional and creative motivation: because we can. Neither artists nor audiences can present works. They require the agency, power, intentionality, and, perhaps, complicity of curators to enter the dynamic field of reception. Perhaps we are in a moment where curatorial practice really does anchor to its Latin *curare*, but in a more direct etymology. Boris Groys suggests that curating may in fact be curing,[2] but for the interventionist curator it must also be as much about confounding and creating. As importantly, it is communicating. But most of all, it must be contextualizing and uncompromising. Situating complex works of contemporary culture within accessible dialogues and creating transparent spaces for their translation and experience from intention to reception, including intervention, must be the goal of curatorial practice today. Transparency means accountability and, with curatorial intervention, the responsibility and acknowledgment of curatorial practices may well create more experiential, more connective, and more philosophical responses to art. Now is the time for the interventionists to be acknowledged, if not necessarily fully revealed. Why? Because we can.

NOTES

1. Lubar, "Curator as Auteur," 71.

2. Groys, "The Curator as Iconoclast," loc. 1000. Groys writes, "Curating is curing. The process of curating cures the image's powerlessness, its incapacity to present itself. The artwork needs external help; it needs an exhibition and a curator to become visible."

Bibliography

Acord, Sophia Krzys. "Beyond the Head: The Practical Work of Curating Contemporary Art." *Qualitative Sociology* 33 (2010): 447–67. https://doi.org/10.1007/s11133-010-9164-y.

———. "Guest Curating in the Museum: Lost in Translation?" *Esse*. Accessed January 13, 2021. https://esse.ca/en/guest-curating-museum-lost-translation.

Alvis, Jason W. "Making Sense of Heidegger's 'Phenomenology of the Inconspicuous' or Inapparent (*Phänomenologie des Unscheinbaren*)." *Continental Philosophy Review* 51 (2018): 211–38. https://doi.org/10.1007/s11007-017-9422-8.

Ames, Eric. "Everyone's a Curator!" *The Baylor Digital Collections Blog* (blog). May 3, 2019. https://blogs.baylor.edu/digitalcollections/2012/05/03/everyones-a-curator/.

Amman, Jean-Christophe, Bazon Brock, and Harald Szeemann, Second Concept for Documenta 5, in Szeemann 2008, 100.

Amundsen, H. B., and G. E. Morland. "Request for a Radical Redefinition: Curatorial Politics after Institutional Critique." In *Curating and Politics Beyond the Curator: Initial Reflections*, edited by H. B. Amundsen and G. E. Morland, 15–28. Berlin: Hatje Cantz, 2015.

Andreotti, Margherita, and Constantin Brancusi. "Brancusi's 'Golden Bird': A New Species of Modern Sculpture." *Art Institute of Chicago Museum Studies* 19, no. 2 (1993): 134–52, 198–203. https://doi.org/10.2307/4108737.

Barbatsis, Gretchen. "Reception Theory." In *Handbook of Visual Communication*, edited by Ken Smith, Sandra Moriarty, Gretchen Barbatsis, and Keith Kenney, 271–94. New York: Routledge, 2004.

Barragán, Paco. "The Curator as Censor (On Censorship and Curating)." *ArtPulse*. Accessed January 13, 2021. http://artpulsemagazine.com/the-curator-as-censor-on-censorship-and-curating.

Batycka, D. "The 9th Berlin Biennale: A Vast Obsolescent Pageant of Irrelevance." *hyperallergic*. Published June 24, 2016. http://hyperallergic.com/306932/the-9th-berlin-biennale-a-vast-obsolescent-pageant-of-irrelevance/.

———. "Art and Creative Acts That Were Censored in 2019." *hyperallergic*. Published January 7, 2020. https://hyperallergic.com/534808/art-and-creative-acts-that-were-censored-in-2019/.

Baudrillard, J. *The Transparency of Evil: Essays on Extreme Phenomena*. London: Verso, 1996.

Benjamin, Walter. "The Work of Art in the Age of Mechanical Reproduction." In *Illuminations: Essays and Reflections*, edited by H. Arendt, 217–51. New York: Schocken Books, 1968.

Berger, Maurice. "Are Art Museums Racist?" *Art in America*. Published March 31, 2020. https://www.artnews.com/art-in-america/features/maurice-berger-are-art-museums-racist-1202682524/.

Bishop, Clare. "What Is a Curator?" *Idea*. Accessed January 13, 2021. http://idea.ro/revista/ro/article/XIpUPRAAACYAyy0X/ce-este-un-curator.

Blazwick, Iwona, S. Cahan, A. Fraser, M. Clegg, M. Guttmann, U. M. Bauer, and S. Dillemuth. "Serving Audiences." *October* 80 (1997): 128–39. https://doi.org/10.2307/778813.

Bonami, Francesco. "Ask a Curator: Francesco Bonami on Difficult Artists, the Decade's Biggest Art Flops, and More." *Artnews*. Published January 8, 2020. https://www.artnews.com/art-news/news/ask-a-curator-francesco-bonami-art-flops-1202

674675.

———. "Francesco Bonami Remembers Late Curator Germano Celant: 'He Changed the Way Art Was Made.'" *Artnews*. Published May 4, 2020. https://www.artnews.com/art-news/news/germano-celant-francesco-bonami-remembrance-1202685819/.

Boucher, Brian. "Whitney Museum Hangs Jackson Pollock Painting the Wrong Way." *Artnet.com*, "News." Published May 4, 2015. https://news.artnet.com/exhibitions/jackson-pollock-sideways-whitney-museum-294233.

Brenson, Michael. "The Curator's Moment." *Art Journal* 57, no. 4 (1998).

Brown, Kate. "'Plexiglass Has Become a Symbol of Care': How a Berlin Museum Reimagined a Participatory Art Show in the Era of Social Distancing." *Artnet.com*, "News." Accessed September 24, 2020. https://news.artnet.com/exhibitions/lee-mingwei-gropius-bau-1862328.

Browne, Kelvin. "A Museum without Visitors Is Just an Attractive Warehouse." *The Globe and Mail*, June 4, 2020. https://www.theglobeandmail.com/arts/art-and-architecture/article-a-museum-without-visitors-is-just-an-attractive-warehouse/.

Cannon-Brookes, Peter. "Impermanence: A Curator's Viewpoint." *Leonardo* 16, no. 1 (1983): 34–35. http://www.jstor.org/stable/1575040.

Cascone, Sarah. "This Day in History: The Museum of Modern Art Hung a Matisse Upside Down and No One Noticed." *Artnet.com*, "News." Published October 18, 2016. https://news.artnet.com/exhibitions/moma-hangs-matisse-upside-down-683900.

Casey, Valerie. "Staging Meaning: Performance in the Modern Museum." *TDR* 49, no. 3 (2005): 78–95.

Chave, Anna. *Constantin Brancusi: Shifting the Bases of Art*. New Haven, CT: Yale University Press, 1994.

Cohen, Alina. "Everyone's a Curator. That's Not (Always) a Bad Thing." *Artsy*. Published December 21, 2018. https://www.artsy.net/article/artsy-editorial-everyones-curator-bad-thing.

Copeland, Colette. "Aural Sensation: Janet Cardiff and George Bures Miller." *Afterimage* 39, no. 4 (2012): 30–31.

Corbett, Rachel. "The End of Exhibitions? As Attendance Plummets, New York Dealers Are Scrambling to Secure the Future of the Art Gallery." *Artnet.com*, "News." Published July 18, 2018. https://news.artnet.com/market/foot-traffic-galleries-new-york-1318769.

Cotter, L. *Curating, Cultural Capital and Symbolic Power: Representations of Irish Art in London, 1950–2010*. PhD diss. University of Amsterdam, 2010. https://pure.uva.nl/ws/files/1426773/85906_thesis.pdf.

Crimp, D. *On the Museum's Ruins*. Cambridge: MIT Press, 1993.

Da Silva, José. "AI You Ready for This? Bucharest Biennale to Be Curated by Artificial Intelligence Called Jarvis." *The Art Newspaper*. Published May 27, 2020. https://www.theartnewspaper.com/news/the-tenth-bucharest-biennale-to-be-curated-by-an-ai-programme-called-jarvis.

De Freitas, Nancy. "Breathing Space for Experience." *The International Journal of the Arts in Society* 6, no. 2 (2011): 305–21.

Derieux, F., and F. Aubart. *Harald Szeemann: Individual Methodology*. Zurich: JRP Ringier Kunstverlag Ag, 2007.

Di Liscia, Valentina, and Hakim Bishara. "Whitney Museum Cancels Show after Artists Denounce Acquisition Process, Citing Exploitation." *hyperallergic*. Published August 25, 2020. https://hyperallergic.com/584340/whitney-museum-black-lives-matter-covid-19-exhibition-canceled/.

Dinoia, Megan. "When Art Is Alive, How Do You Conserve It?" *Iris Blog* (blog), December 11, 2019. https://blogs.getty.edu/iris/when-art-is-alive-how-do-you-conserve-it/.

Dunn, Megan, and Ronnie van Hout. "Bad Dads: An Interview with Ronnie van Hout and Megan Dunn." *Eyeline* 91 (2019): 42–49.

Edgers, Geoff. "Behind Doors, a World Unseen." *Boston Globe*. March 28, 2007. Accessed January 6, 2019. http://archive.boston.com/ae/theater_arts/articles/2007/03/28/behind_doors_a_world_unseen/?page=2.

———. "Dismantled." *Boston Globe*, October 21, 2007. http://archive.boston.com/ae/theater_arts/articles/2007/10/21/dismantled/.

Elbaor, Caroline. "Getting a Master's Degree in Curating Is All the Rage. But Is It Worth It?" *Artnet.com*, "News." Published July 5, 2017. https://news.artnet.com/art-world/are-masters-degrees-in-curating-worth-it-986090.

Fabrikant, Geraldine. "The Good Stuff in the Back Room." *New York Times*, March 12, 2009. https://www.nytimes.com/2009/03/19/arts/artsspecial/19TROVE.html.

Farquharson, A. "Curator and Artist: The Art of Performative Curating." *Art Monthly* 9, no. 3 (2003): 7–10. https://www.artmonthly.co.uk/magazine/site/article/curator-and-artist-by-alex-farquharson-october-2003.

Fotiadi, Eva. "The Canon of the Author." *Journal of Art Historiography* 11 (2014). https://arthistoriography.files.wordpress.com/2014/11/fotiadi.pdf.

Foucault, Michel. "What Is an Author?" In *Language, Counter-Memory, Practice*, edited by Donald F. Bouchard. Translated by Donald F. Bouchard and Sherry Simon. Ithaca, NY: Cornell University Press, 1977.

Fowle, K. "Who Cares: Understanding the Role of the Curator Today." In *Cautionary Tales: Critical Curating*, edited by S. Rand and H. Kouris, 9–12. New York: Apexart, 2007.

Fox, Dan. "Being Curated." *Frieze*. Published April 13, 2013. https://frieze.com/article/being-curated.

Gadamer, H. *Truth and Method*. New York: Bloomsbury Academic, 2014. Kindle Edition.

Gamerman, Ellen. "Everybody's an Art Curator." *Wall Street Journal*, October 23, 2014. https://www.wsj.com/articles/everybodys-an-art-curator-1414102402.

Gaskell, I. "Being True to Artists." *Journal of Aesthetics and Art Criticism* 61, no. 1 (2003): 53–60. http://www.jstor.org/stable/1559113.

Gillick, Liam. "The Complete Curator." In *Curating Research*, edited by Paul O'Neill and Mick Wilson, 24–31. London: Open Editions/de Appel, 2015.

Goldstein, Andrew. "So, Is MoMA Woke Now? Not Quite. A Q&A with Director Glenn Lowry on Why 'You Can Never Be Comprehensive in Some Absolute Way.'" *Artnet.com*, "News." Published October 15, 2019. https://news.artnet.com/the-big-interview/glenn-lowry-moma-reopening-interview-part-1-1678816.

Gover, K. E. "Christoph Büchel v. Mass MoCA: A Tilted Arc for the Twenty-First Century." *Journal of Aesthetic Education* 46, no. 1 (2012): 46–58.

Greenberger, Alex. "5 Essential Exhibitions by Germano Celant, Late Curator Who Coined Arte Povera." *Artnews.com*. Published April 30, 2020. https://www.artnews.com/art-news/news/germano-celant-essential-exhibitions-1202685358/.

Groys, Boris. "The Curator as Iconoclast." In *Cautionary Tales: Critical Curating*, edited by Steven Rand, loc. 1000. New York: Apex Art, 2010. Kindle Edition.

Harrison, Robert Pogue. "A Messenger of the Rope: In Conversation with Peter Sloterdijk." *The Los Angeles Review of Books*. Published July 10, 2019. https://lareviewofbooks.org/article/a-messenger-of-the-rope-in-conversation-with-peter-sloterdijk/.

Heiferman, Marvin. "Everyone's a Curator, Now." Smithsonian Institution Archives. Published November 15, 2010. https://siarchives.si.edu/blog/everyones-curator-now.

Hendeles, Ydessa. "Curatorial Compositions." In *The Exhibitionist: Journal on Exhibition Making, the First Six Years*, edited by Jens Hoffmann, 361–66. New York: The Exhibitionist, 2012.

Higgs, Matthew. "Between the Audience and the Stage." In *The Edge of Everything: Reflections on Curatorial Practice*, edited by Catherine Thomas, 15–22. New York: Walter Phillips Gallery, 2002.

Hoffmann, Jens. "Overture." In *The Exhibitionist: Journal on Exhibition Making, the First Six Years*, edited by Jens Hoffmann, 29–30. New York: The Exhibitionist, 2017.

InVisible Culture. "Amending Rachel Whiteread's Water Tower: Infrastructure as Art, Art as Infrastructure." Published October 29, 2015. https://ivc.lib.rochester.edu/amending-rachel-whitereads-water-tower-infrastructure-as-art-art-as-infrastructure/.

Iser, W. *The Act of Reading: A Theory of Aesthetic Response*. Baltimore: Johns Hopkins University Press, 1978.

Jauss, H. R. *Theory and History of Literature: Aesthetic Experience and Literary Hermeneutics*. Vol. 3. Minneapolis, MN: University of Minnesota Press, 1982.

———. *Theory and History of Literature: Towards an Aesthetic of Reception*. Vol. 2. Minneapolis, MN: University of Minnesota Press, 1982.

Kafka, Franz. "Before the Law." *Kafka Online*. Accessed October 4, 2020. https://www.kafka-online.info/before-the-law.html.

Kaplan, Isaac. "When Collectors—Not Curators—Dictate Art History." *Artsy*. Published June 29, 2017. https://www.artsy.net/article/artsy-editorial-collectors-curators-dictate-art-history.

Kemp, W. "The Work of Art and Its Beholder: The Methodology and Aesthetic of Reception." In *The Subjects of Art History: Historical Objects in Contemporary Perspectives*, edited by M. Cheetham, M. Holly, and K. Moxey, 180–96. Cambridge: Cambridge University Press, 1998.

Kennedy, Randy. "Artists Rights Act Applies in Dispute, Court Rules." *New York Times*, January 28, 2010. https://www.nytimes.com/2010/01/29/arts/design/29artist.html.

Kenney, Nancy. "After Controversial Cancellation in Cleveland, Mass MoCA Will Exhibit Shaun Leonardo's Images of Black Victims." *The Art Newspaper*. Accessed January 13, 2021. https://www.theartnewspaper.com/news/after-controversial-cancellation-in-cleveland-mass-moca-will-host-exhibition-of-shaun-leonardo-s-works-depicting-black-us-victims.

King, Natalie. "Primavera 1994." Museum of Contemporary Art, unpaginated.

Kingston, Anne. "Everyone's a Curator Now." *Maclean's*. Published October 20, 2011. https://www.macleans.ca/culture/have-you-curated-your-wrist-yet/.

Leonard, Robert. "Stella Brennan: History Curator." Accessed January 13, 2021. https://robertleonard.org/history-curator/.

Lind, Maria. "On the Curatorial," *Artforum* 48, no. 2 (2009), 103.

———. "Why Mediate Art?" In *Ten Fundamental Questions of Curating*, edited by Jens Hoffmann, loc. 1318–22. Mousse Publishing, 2013. Kindle Edition.

Lubar, Steven. "Curator as Auteur." *The Public Historian* 36, no. 1 (2014): 71–76.

Mara de Wachter, Ellen. "After the Nymphs Painting Backlash: Is Curatorial Activism a Right or an Obligation?" *Frieze*. Published February 7, 2018. https://www.frieze.com/article/after-nymphs-painting-backlash-curatorial-activism-right-or-obligation.

Marincola, P., P. T. Nesbett, and S. McEneaney. *Pigeons on the Grass Alas: Contemporary Curators Talk about the Field*. Philadelphia: Pew Center for Arts and Heritage, 2013.

Marshall, Christopher R. "Ghosts in the Machine: The Artistic Intervention as a Site of Museum Collaboration–Accommodation in Recent Curatorial Practice." *International Journal of the Inclusive Museum* 4, no. 2 (2012): 65–80.

Martinon, Jean-Paul. *Curating as Ethics*. Minneapolis: University of Minnesota Press, 2020.

Metropolitan Museum of Art. "General Information." Accessed October 1, 2020. https://www.metmuseum.org/press/general-information?&st=facet&&rpp=10&pg=1.

Micchelli, Thomas. "Christoph Büchel, *Training Ground for Democracy*." The Brooklyn Rail. Accessed January 13, 2021. https://brooklynrail.org/2007/09/artseen/buchel.

Mitchell, Jennifer Anne. "A Smithsonian Curator Opens Up about Artwork and How Her Own Work Has Changed during the Pandemic." *Washington City Paper*. Accessed September 19, 2020. https://washingtoncitypaper.com/article/303993/a-smithsonian-curator-opens-up-about-artwork-and-how-her-own-work-has-changed-during-the-pandemic/.

Molesworth, Helen. "The Kids Are Always Alright: Helen Molesworth on the Reinstallation of MoMA's Permanent Collection." *Artforum* 58, no. 5 (2020).

Morris, Robert. "Regarding Documenta V." Flash Art, 1972. https://flash---art.com/article/robert-morris/.

Muchnic, Suzanne. "Van Gogh Painting Sells at Record $82.5 Million: Art: 'Portrait of Dr. Gachet' Is Auctioned to a Japanese Gallery. The Previous High Price Was $53.9 Million." *Los Angeles Times,* May 16, 1990. https://www.latimes.com/archives/la-xpm-1990-05-16-mn-262-story.html.

National Coalition Against Censorship. "Art and Culture Censorship Timeline." Accessed January 13, 2021. https://ncac.org/resource/art-and-culture-censorship-timeline.

Neuendorf, Henri. "Art Demystified: What Do Curators Actually Do?" *Artnet.com,* "News." Published November 10, 2016. https://news.artnet.com/art-world/art-demystified-curators-741806.

———. "Francesco Bonami Says Curators Are 'Self-Delusional' and 'Irrelevant' in Today's Art World." *Artnet.com,* "News." Published June 7, 2016. https://news.artnet.com/market/francesco-bonami-says-curators-self-delusional-irrelevant-todays-art-world-512705.

Nietzsche, Friedrich. *On the Genealogy of Morals*. Project Gutenberg. Accessed January 13, 2021. https://www.gutenberg.org/files/52319/52319-h/52319-h.htm.

Obrist, Hans-Ulrich. "Mind over Matter." 1996. *Radical Matters*. Accessed October 13, 2020. http://www.radicalmatters.com/metasound/pdf/harald_szeemann-mind_over_matter_by_hans-ulrich_obrist.pdf.

Obrist, Hans Ulrich. *A Brief History of Curating*. Zurich: JRP/Ringier, 2008.

Obrist, Hans Ulrich and Harald Szeemann (1996) Curator Interview. Artforum. https://www.artforum.com/print/199609/curator-interview-33047.

O'Doherty, Brian. *Inside the White Cube: The Ideology of the Gallery Space*. Berkeley: University of California Press, 1986.

O'Neill, Paul. "The Co-Dependent Curator." *Art Monthly*. Accessed January 13, 2021. https://www.artmonthly.co.uk/magazine/site/article/the-co-dependent-curator-by-paul-oneill-november-2005.

———. "Co-Productive Exhibition-Making and Three Principal Categories of Organisation: The Background, the Middle-Ground and the Foreground." *On Curating*. Published April 22, 2014. http://www.on-curating.org/issue-22-43/co-productive-exhibition-making-and-three-principal-categories-of-organisation-the-background-the-middle-ground-and-the-foregrou.html#.Wbn0S4px2Ho.

———. *The Culture of Curating and the Curating of Culture(s)*. Cambridge, MA: The MIT Press, 2012.

O'Neill, P., M. Wilson, and L. Steeds. *The Curatorial Conundrum: What to Study? What to Research? What to Practice?* Cambridge, MA: MIT Press, 2016.

Palermo, Charles. "Introduction: Intention and Interpretation." *Nonsite.org*. Published July 1, 2012. https://nonsite.org/introduction-intention-and-interpretation/.

Pappas, George. "Internalist vs. Externalist Conceptions of Epistemic Justification." *Stanford Encyclopedia of Philosophy*. Fall 2017 edition. https://plato.stanford.edu/entries/justep-intext/.

Pogrebin, Robin, and Scott Reyburn. "A Basquiat Sells for 'Mind-Blowing' $110.5 Million at Auction." *New York Times,* May 18, 2017. https://www.nytimes.com/2017/05/18/arts/jean-michel-basquiat-painting-is-sold-for-110-million-at-auction.html.

Reilly, Maura. "What Is Curatorial Activism?" *Artnews.com*. Published November 7, 2017. https://www.artnews.com/art-news/news/what-is-curatorial-activism-9271/.

———. "MoMA's Revisionism Is Piecemeal and Problem-Filled: Feminist Art Historian Maura Reilly on the Museum's Rehang." *Artnews.com*. Published October 31, 2019. https://www.artnews.com/art-news/reviews/moma-rehang-art-historian-mau

ra-reilly-13484/.

Richman-Abdou, Kelly. "What Is Curating? See Why More and More People Are Interested in Becoming Curators." *My Modern Met*. Published August 1, 2019. https://mymodernmet.com/what-is-curating/.

Richter, Dorothee. "On Artistic and Curatorial Authorship," *On Curating* 19 (2013), 45.

Saltz, Jerry. "The Alchemy of Curating." *Artnet.com*. Accessed January 13, 2021. http://www.artnet.com/magazineus/features/saltz/saltz7-17-07.asp.

Sayej, Nadja. "J Marion Sims: Controversial Statue Taken Down but Debate Still Rages." *The Guardian*, April 21, 2018. https://www.theguardian.com/artanddesign/2018/apr/21/j-marion-sims-statue-removed-new-york-city-black-women.

SBS News. "Biennale of Sydney Cuts Ties with Sponsor Transfield." Update July 3, 2014. http://www.sbs.com.au/news/article/2014/03/07/biennale-sydney-cuts-ties-sponsor-transfield.

Schechner, R. "Ways of Speaking, Loci of Cognition." *TDR* 31, no. 3 (1987): 4–7. http://www.jstor.org/stable/1145791.

Schjeldahl, Peter. "The Exuberance of MoMA's Expansion." *The New Yorker*. Published October 14, 2019. https://www.newyorker.com/magazine/2019/10/21/the-exuberance-of-momas-expansion.

Sheikh, Simon. "From Para to Post: The Rise and Fall of Curatorial Reason." *Springerin* 1 (2017). https://www.springerin.at/en/2017/1/von-para-zu-post/.

———. "The Potential of Curatorial Articulation." *On Curating* 4 (2010): 4–6.

Simon, Nina. "Self-Censorship for Museum Professionals." *Museum 2.0* (blog). October 22, 2008. http://museumtwo.blogspot.com/2008/10/self-censorship-for-museum.html.

Smith, Ken, Sandra Moriarty, Gretchen Barbatsis, and Keith Kenney, eds. *Handbook of Visual Communication*. New York: Routledge, 2004.

Smith, Terry. *Thinking Contemporary Curating*. New York, NY: Independent Curators International, 2013.

———. "Interview with Clare Bishop." In *Talking Contemporary Curating*, edited by Kate Fowle and Leigh Markopoulos. New York: Independent Curators International, 2015.

Solway, Diane. "Picasso Mania." *W* (*wmagazine.com*). October 27, 2015. https://www.wmagazine.com/gallery/picasso-mania-exhibition/.

Spaid, Sue. (2016). Revisiting Ventzislavov's thesis: "Curating should be understood as a fine art." *Journal of Aesthetics and Art Criticism*, 74 (1), 87.

Stainforth, Elizabeth, and Glyn Thompson. "Curatorial 'Translations': The Case of Marcel Duchamp's Green Box." *Journal of Curatorial Studies* 5, no. 2 (2016): 238–55. https://doi.org/10.1386/jcs.5.2.238_1.

Storr, R. "How We Do What We Do. And How We Don't." In *Curating Now: Imaginative Practice, Public Responsibility*, edited by Paula Marincola. Philadelphia: Philadelphia Exhibitions Initiative, 2001.

Szeemann, Harald. "First Exhibition Concepts for Documenta 5," in Szeemann 2008, 95.

Thea, Carolee. *Foci: Interviews with Ten International Curators*. New York: Apex Art, 2001.

———. "Nzewi, Ugochukwu-Smooth." In *On Curating 2: Paradigm Shifts, Interviews with Fourteen International Curators*. New York: Distributed Art Publishers, 2016.

Thea, Carolee, and T. Micchelli. *On Curating: Interviews with Ten International Curators*. New York: Distributed Art Publishers, 2009.

Troemel, Brad. "The Accidental Audience." *The New Enquiry*. Published March 14, 2013. https://thenewinquiry.com/the-accidental-audience/.

Urist, Jacoba. "How Do You Conserve Artworks Made of Bologna, or Bubble Gum, or Soap?" *The Atlantic*, June 9, 2017. https://www.theatlantic.com/science/archive/2017/06/how-do-you-conserve-art-made-of-bologna-or-bubble-gum-or-soap/529713/.

Vedantam, Shankar. "Remembering Anarcha, Lucy, and Betsey: The Mothers of Modern Gynecology." *Hidden Brain*. February 16, 2016. https://www.npr.org/transcripts/466942135.

Ventzislavov, Rossen. (2014). "Idle arts: Reconsidering the curator." *Journal of Aesthetics and Art Criticism*, 72 (1), 83.

———. (2016). "The Curator as Artist: Reply to Sue Spaid." *Journal of Aesthetics and Art Criticism*, 74 (1), 92.

Vidokle, Anton. "Art without Artists." *E-flux.com*. Accessed September 25, 2020. http://worker01.eflux.com/pdf/article_136.pdf.

———. "Art without Market, Art without Education: Political Economy of Art." *E-flux.com*. Accessed January 13, 2021. http://www.e-flux.com/journal/43/60205/art-without-market-art-without-education-political-economy-of-art/.

Vogel, Felix. "Authorship as Legitimation." Accessed January 13, 2021. https://edoc.unibas.ch/61198/1/Autorschaft%20als%20Legitimation.pdf.

von Bismarck, Beatrice. "'The Master of the Works': Daniel Buren's Contribution to *documenta 5* in Kassel, 1972." *On Curating* 33 (2017). https://www.on-curating.org/issue-33-reader/the-master-of-the-works-daniel-burens-contribution-to-documenta-5-in-kassel-1972.html#.X4Yl2i9h01I.

Waterson, Jim. "Saatchi Gallery Covers Up Artworks after Muslim Visitors' Complaints." *The Guardian*, May 5, 2019. https://www.theguardian.com/artanddesign/2019/may/05/saatchi-covers-up-artworks-after-complaints-by-muslim-visitors.

Linda Weintraub (2013). "Curatorial Flow Patterns." Reprinted at lindaweintraub.com. http://lindaweintraub.com/curatorial-flow-patterns/.

Weisman, Steven. "Japanese Translator of Rushdie Book Found Slain." *New York Times*, July 13, 1991. https://archive.nytimes.com/www.nytimes.com/books/99/04/18/specials/rushdie-translator.html?mcubz=0.

Wells, Liz. "Curatorial Strategy as Critical Intervention: The Genesis of Facing East." Accessed January 13, 2021. https://mcn2018.files.wordpress.com/2017/12/curatorial-strategy-as-critical-intervention-the-genesis-of-facing-east_-in-rugg-j-and-sedgwick-m.pdf.

Zangwill, Nick. "Art and Audience." *Journal of Aesthetics and Art Criticism* 57, no. 3 (1999): 313–32. https://www.jstor.org/stable/432197.

Zaragoza, Alex. "The Whitney Museum Pillaging Works by Black Artists Is Nothing New." *Vice*. Published August 28, 2020. https://www.vice.com/en/article/n7wm9b/the-whitney-museum-pillaging-black-art-from-see-in-black-is-nothing-new.

Zerocv, B. "An Interview with Daniel Buren." *Manifesta* 5 (2005): 160–75.

Index

agency: and intervention, 4, 10, 120
artistic, 15, 23, 25, 52, 65, 84, 86, 89
authorial, 91; curatorial, 1, 2, 10, 19n57, 30, 31, 33, 34, 35, 37, 40, 48, 50, 63, 65, 72, 84, 88, 89, 95, 97, 98, 110, 116, 120, 124; institutional, 24
Andrews, Gail, 109, 110, 115, 120
architecture, 9, 31, 94, 116
artist's rights, 24

Benjamin, Walter, 55, 83
Bishop, Claire, 2, 63, 65
Brennan, Stella, 83
Broodthaers, Marcel, 51
Buckley, Brad, 56, 69, 88
Buren, Daniel, 30, 45, 46, 57

Duchamp, Marcel, 13, 31, 40

film, 14, 39, 52, 95, 100
Friend, Reuben, 115, 116, 117, 120
Foucault, Michel, 3–4, 13, 49

Guoriotis, Kon, 113, 114–115, 120

Heidegger, Martin, 4, 30, 41, 92
hierarchy: curator-artist-audience, 29; curatorial hierarchy, 49, 93, 107; institutional hierarchy, 99, 107; of objects, 10; of values, 26
Hoover, Justin, 96, 97, 97–98, 101

installation, 8, 9, 21, 22, 24, 26, 33, 37, 38, 42n14, 47, 50–53, 63, 69, 75, 76, 77, 78, 80, 85, 88, 89, 89n8, 92, 95, 124

Jauss, Hans Robert, 3, 4, 11, 12–13, 54, 55, 87
Johnston, Courtney, 95, 111, 117

Kessell, Mark, 83, 86, 87, 87–88

Leonard, Robert, 62, 63, 65, 69, 83, 93, 94, 95, 101
Lerner, Adam, 70, 108, 115
Lewis, Ruark, 94

Maori, 16, 45, 96, 98
Martinon, Jean-Paul, 3, 6, 56
Massachusetts Museum of Contemporary Art (MASS MoCA), 21, 22, 23, 24, 25, 26, 40, 41n2, 41n3, 41n11, 42n13

Nietzsche, Friedrich, 27, 55, 64

Obrist, Hans Ulrich, 2, 6

painting, viii, 2, 7, 14, 23, 30, 38, 49, 52, 84, 92, 102n4, 105, 106, 107, 109, 114, 115, 117, 121n8, 124
phenomenology, 41, 76
photograph, 14, 105, 112
photography/photographer, 14, 45, 83
photographic, 10, 29, 55

reception theory, 3, 4, 11, 12, 13, 14, 33, 34, 50, 55, 124
Rinder, Lawrence, 12, 119, 120
Ross Smith, Bayeté, 50–51, 58, 80–81, 82–83, 88

Seeto, Aaron, 64, 65, 93, 94, 95, 100, 101, 102
site-specific, 21
Smith, Ross T., 16, 45, 46, 50, 80, 86, 87, 88
Smith, Terry, 2, 37
Suparak, Astria, 94–95, 96, 100–101, 101

Szeemann, Harald, 27–30, 31, 37, 42n27, 45, 63, 67, 70, 79

Tamati-Quennell, Megan, 96, 98, 99, 101, 102

Van Hout, Ronnie, 53, 57–58, 82

About the Author

Brett M. Levine is a curator, writer, and editor who explores the intersections between intentionality, interventionality, and reception. Formerly the director of Lopdell House Gallery, Auckland, and team leader of the collection programs at the Dowse Art Museum, Wellington, Levine's curatorial projects explore questions of representation, identity, and perception with an emphasis on installation, time-based media, and experimental practices. His writings have appeared in *Art New Zealand*, *Object*, *Urbis*, and *Art Papers* as well as in monographs on Brad Buckley and Ross T. Smith. Levine lives and works in Birmingham, Alabama.